Cambridge Elements

Elements in International Relations
edited by
Jon C. W. Pevehouse
University of Wisconsin–Madison
Tanja A. Börzel
Freie Universität Berlin
Edward D. Mansfield
University of Pennsylvania

WHEN HEDGING FAILS

Structural Uncertainty, Protective Options, and Geopolitical (Im)Prudence in Smaller Powers' Behaviour

Alexander Korolev
The University of New South Wales

Shaftesbury Road, Cambridge CB2 8EA, United Kingdom

One Liberty Plaza, 20th Floor, New York, NY 10006, USA

477 Williamstown Road, Port Melbourne, VIC 3207, Australia

314–321, 3rd Floor, Plot 3, Splendor Forum, Jasola District Centre,
New Delhi – 110025, India

103 Penang Road, #05–06/07, Visioncrest Commercial, Singapore 238467

Cambridge University Press is part of Cambridge University Press & Assessment,
a department of the University of Cambridge.

We share the University's mission to contribute to society through the pursuit of
education, learning and research at the highest international levels of excellence.

www.cambridge.org
Information on this title: www.cambridge.org/9781009638081
DOI: 10.1017/9781009638050

© Alexander Korolev 2025

This publication is in copyright. Subject to statutory exception and to the provisions
of relevant collective licensing agreements, no reproduction of any part may take
place without the written permission of Cambridge University Press & Assessment.

When citing this work, please include a reference to the DOI 10.1017/9781009638050

First published 2025

A catalogue record for this publication is available from the British Library

ISBN 978-1-009-63808-1 Hardback
ISBN 978-1-009-63806-7 Paperback
ISSN 2515-706X (online)
ISSN 2515-7302 (print)

Cambridge University Press & Assessment has no responsibility for the persistence
or accuracy of URLs for external or third-party internet websites referred to in this
publication and does not guarantee that any content on such websites is, or will remain,
accurate or appropriate.

For EU product safety concerns, contact us at Calle de José Abascal, 56, 1°, 28003
Madrid, Spain, or email eugpsr@cambridge.org

When Hedging Fails

Structural Uncertainty, Protective Options, and Geopolitical (Im)Prudence in Smaller Powers' Behaviour

Elements in International Relations

DOI: 10.1017/9781009638050
First published online: December 2025

Alexander Korolev
The University of New South Wales
Author for correspondence: Alexander Korolev, a.korolev@unsw.edu.au

Abstract: Hedging has been widely viewed as an optimal foreign policy for small and middle powers. However, hedging was more effective in some cases than others and ultimately proved detrimental for certain states. This Element contributes to knowledge about hedging by explaining why some smaller powers can hedge successfully between competing great powers while others fail, suffering serious harm. It develops a theoretical model consisting of international-systemic and state-level variables that determine hedging outcomes. It then tests the model using cases in the post-Soviet space (Georgia, Ukraine) and Southeast Asia (Malaysia, Vietnam, the Philippines) exposed to great power rivalry but exhibiting different hedging outcomes. It shows that hedging failure occurs due to changes in three key variables – structural uncertainty, availability of protective options, and decision-makers' geopolitical prudence – and interactions between them. The Element highlights the limits to smaller power hedging and argues that hedging should not be taken for granted.

Keywords: hedging, balancing, great power rivalry, structural uncertainty, prudence

© Alexander Korolev 2025

ISBNs: 9781009638081 (HB), 9781009638067 (PB), 9781009638050 (OC)
ISSNs: 2515-706X (online), 2515-7302 (print)

Contents

1 Introduction 1

2 Theoretical Framework: Why Hedging Fails 3

3 Structure, Protective Options, and Geopolitical (Im)Prudence: Georgia and Ukraine 21

4 Sustaining Hedging in Southeast Asia: The Philippines, Vietnam, and Malaysia 34

5 Conclusion 49

References 51

1 Introduction

Much attention in the literature on hedging has focused on ascertaining, categorizing, and explaining different patterns of hedging behaviour (Goh, 2006; Chung, 2009; Jackson, 2014; Lim & Cooper, 2015; Koga, 2018; Chan, 2019; Haacke, 2019; Kuik, 2021; Chang, 2022). However, there has been little systematic work on why hedging might fail. Very few studies have touched upon the problem of unsuccessful hedging (Ciorciari, 2019; Korolev, 2019; Smith, 2020), and none have systematically explored the causes of hedging failure. Meanwhile, hedging does fail, becomes more difficult, or goes awry to various degrees across many different cases – from the Philippines and Vietnam in Southeast Asia (Ciorciari, 2019) to Georgia and Ukraine in the post-Soviet space (Korolev, 2019; Smith, 2020), and to even Australia (White, 2009) – thus presenting a cautionary tale against the potential pitfalls of hedging. For small and middle powers, the question of why hedging fails and how to hedge to avert harm from mightier great powers is often a question of survival, thus highlighting the importance of understanding why hedging strategies fail and succeed.

This Element attempts to fill this knowledge gap. It defines successful and unsuccessful hedging and explains why some smaller powers can hedge relatively successfully between competing great powers while others fail to and suffer serious harm. The goal is not to deliver an exhaustive list of causal factors that affect hedging outcomes but to develop and test a theory-grounded baseline model that can help understand the success and failure of hedging. The suggested model highlights the importance of three critical causal variables – structural uncertainty, availability of protective options, and decision-maker's geopolitical prudence – and their relationship in determining hedging outcomes. It defines these three variables and elaborates how changes in and between them affect hedging under the conditions of intensifying great power rivalry.

The Element also argues that the three causal variables are related to one another – they are dynamically correlated. The level of structural uncertainty is the independent variable that sets up the context for and conditions the role of the other two variables in determining smaller powers' hedging outcomes. Specifically, high structural uncertainty is associated with a less determined balance of power dynamics and lower systemic pressure. Hedging becomes easy, the need for protective options less urgent, and the costs of geopolitical imprudence lower. When structural uncertainty disappears and balancing between great powers intensifies, the stakes involved in hedging rise dramatically as hedging smaller powers come under the pressure of acute strategic dilemmas. This growing external pressure increases the need for adequate protective options, the cultivation of which becomes an important component of smaller power hedging behaviour and a mediator of structural uncertainty's impact on hedging outcomes. However, such protective options become surrounded by greater strategic complexity that smaller states must navigate. These changes make the costs of mistakes unaffordable and require more prudence in assessing both the structural environment and the availability of projective options. Leadership's geopolitical prudence becomes a critical asset that moderates the impact of both structure and protective options on hedging. As the analysis in Section 3 demonstrates, such prudence can be in significant shortage, which increases the dangers of hedging failure.[1]

The analysis proceeds as follows. Section 2 defines the success and failure of hedging (the dependent variable), presents the causal model, and operationalizes its variables. Sections 3 and 4 test the model by probing it across different cases. Section 3 focuses on the post-Soviet space and comprises two cases of failed hedging – Georgia under Michail Saakashvili (2004–2013) and Ukraine during Viktor Yanukovych (2010–2014), while also covering Ukraine's problems with access to protective options after Russia's invasion in 2022. It demonstrates how the two post-Soviet countries' hedging between increasingly competitive Russia and the West became unsuccessful, causing significant harm to their sovereignty and resulting in an eventual shift to balancing against Russia. Section 4 examines Southeast Asia to understand how the situations around structural uncertainty, protective options, and leaders' geopolitical prudence allowed Vietnam, Malaysia, and the Philippines to hedge amidst intensifying China–US rivalry. It shows that while hedging in this region also became more challenging, the three Southeast Asian states continued to hedge and managed not to explicitly choose between the two competing great powers, maintaining territorial integrity and relative strategic autonomy. Section 5 concludes by pulling the strands of the analysis together and suggesting directions for future research.

Methodologically, this research resembles what Eckstein (1991) calls a 'plausibility probe' and Lijphart (1971) – a 'theory-confirming case study'. More precisely, it is a 'series of plausibility probes' (George, 1979) consisting of five case studies to achieve the cumulation of findings. While such an approach falls short of rigorous hypothesis testing in statistical terms, it is useful for determining the potential validity of an initial theoretical model

---

[1] In statistical terms, the character of the theory presented in this study can best be described as a 'moderated mediation model', in which a moderator variable (geopolitical prudence in our case) moderates the relationship between the independent variable (structural uncertainty) and the dependent variable (hedging outcome) while at the same time moderating the relationship between the mediating variable (access to protective option) and the dependent variable (see Figure 1 and associated elaboration next).

(Eckstein, 1991, p. 147). Both the differences and similarities among the cases matter, and cases are selected to establish variance in both dependent and independent variables (George, 1979, p. 209). Therefore, this study selects cases to compare the instances of hedging failure with those of relative success. It first holds the dependent variable constant by studying the cases of hedging failure (Georgia and Ukraine) to identify the causal variables associated with it. Then, the outcome variable is varied by looking at relative hedging success (Malaysia, Vietnam, and the Philippines) to test the conditions of the causal variables that account for this different outcome. Given the goals of this article, more space is given to the failed hedging in Georgia and Ukraine. The three Southeast Asian cases are discussed in lesser detail to identify the changes in the causal variables, if any.

2 Theoretical Framework: Why Hedging Fails

Hedging has been viewed as a state behaviour that does not fit into the categories of 'balancing' and 'bandwagoning' because hedgers avoid explicitly siding with one larger power against another (Goh, 2006; Korolev, 2019; Kuik, 2021). Some viewed hedging as a multidimensional and multi-vectored 'alignment posture' in which mixed strategies of balancing and engagement co-occur in different policy sectors (Wilkins, 2021, pp. 9–10). Hedging is a risk-management 'insurance policy' helping smaller states survives the strategic uncertainty of great power politics (Haacke, 2019; Lai & Kuik, 2020). It is also believed to go beyond standoffish neutrality to include proactive multi-vector engagements (Haacke, 2019; Chang, 2022). Some key features of hedging include equidistant engagements, simultaneousness, and counteracting 'engage-and-resist' measures, characterized by alignment ambiguity and displays of deference and defiance (Jackson, 2014; Koga, 2018; Lim & Cooper, 2015).

As such, hedging is not easy to pin down empirically. Not always a result of well-calculated long-term plans or policies, hedging is rarely advertised in official documents or statements. States prefer to dissociate themselves from hedging due to the poor reputation of the term in the policy community, which is why hedging has remained 'a policy that is implemented without pronouncement' (Kuik, 2021, p. 2). There may be no straightforward and observable decision to hedge or not to hedge faced by decision-makers because foreign policy is a fluid and evolving series of mini-decisions, which utility-maximizing models cannot adequately capture (Marston, 2024, pp. 34–35). This makes hedging less a policy by a concrete traceable decision indicating the onset of hedging and more a risk-management posture that fills the gap between unequivocal alignment and outright opposition, widely adopted by smaller powers facing uncertainty (Jones & Jenne, 2021).

Hedging has been observed to become the most prevalent pattern of smaller powers' behaviour in the uncertain post-Cold War international politics. It has become a central tendency in East and Southeast Asian international relations (Goh, 2006; Chung, 2009; Jackson, 2014, p. 333), with the concept of hedging becoming 'one of the most influential concepts' in the scholarship on the international relations of the twenty-first century Asia-Pacific (Ciorciari & Haacke, 2019, p. 368). It is now routinely observed as a logical, if not inevitable, behaviour of smaller powers in other regions, including the post-Soviet space, the Persian Gulf, and elsewhere (Garlick & Havlová, 2020; Ohle, Cook, & Han, 2020; Smith, 2020).

Meanwhile, literature focusing on the causes of hedging success and failure is scant. Three studies – Ciorciari (2019), Korolev (2019), and Smith (2020) – have scratched the surface of the problem from different perspectives, trying to outline some international-systemic and domestic conditions that may cause hedging failure. However, the definition of hedging failure and the variables that cause hedging to succeed or fail, as well as the relationship between them, have not been specified, making it hard to devise credible empirical tests of the authors' arguments.

Indeed, measuring the success and failure of hedging is not easy because 'effective hedging strategies often contribute to non-events' (Ciorciari, 2019, p. 527). A careful read of the existing literature suggests that successful hedging is generally expected to avert major harm and increase security by minimizing risks vis-à-vis the hedging targets (Jackson, 2014; Ciorciari, 2019; Gerstl, 2022, pp. 20–24). It also helps maintain diplomatic flexibility and autonomy through diversifying stakes and policy options, and helps avoid over-reliance on one power/foreign protector (Jackson, 2014; Koga, 2018; Lai & Kuik, 2020). Successful hedging serves to reap political, economic, or security benefits from the hedging targets while minimizing risks in the same areas (Jackson, 2014; Gerstl, 2022). It helps smaller powers secure advantageous strategic positions while keeping fall-back protective option(s) open for a worst-case scenario (Jackson, 2014; Koga, 2018; Lai & Kuik, 2020). Smaller states developing robust relationships with competing great powers and cultivating maximum protection under the condition of great power rivalry are indications of successful hedging. At the same time, hedging helps 'avoid to align' or, more precisely, 'to be forced to align' (Gerstl, 2022, p. 112). Success is also understood as effective engagement with foreign partners and preparedness for potential challenges (Lai & Kuik, 2020).

Failed hedging, therefore, can be envisaged as the opposite. It happens when, despite all the efforts, serious harm to smaller states' security is not averted. More specifically, when hedging fails, the range of feasible policy options shrinks; diversification efforts fail or result in less advantageous strategic positions; reliance on more powerful external protectors increases or reaches the level of complete dependence that undermines a smaller state's relations with another great power; foreign policy autonomy and diplomatic flexibility decrease; and fall-back options disappear in the times when risks associated with great powers politics turn into imminent security threats. All these adverse outcomes force a smaller power to take an undesirable course of action from the standpoint of security, economic independence, and autonomous decision-making. In the worst-case scenario, hedging failure can result in significant harm in the form of subservience, abandonment, economic insecurity, entrapment in great-power conflicts, domestic authority erosion, the loss of effective sovereignty over territory, and severe damage to or destruction of statehood.

Considering this analysis, a useful way to think about hedging effectiveness is by framing it in terms of security and autonomy – that is, hedging is successful to the extent that the hedger can both avoid suffering serious security losses (such as territory) and manage to remain 'above the fray' in great power competition. These considerations run parallel to the traditional understanding of overarching state security, which Wolfers (1952, pp. 484–489) summarized as some degree of protection of a nation's previously acquired 'two minimum national core values' that all nations have historically sought to preserve: national independence and territorial integrity, which often reappear in the later literature as 'autonomy' and 'survival' (Waltz, 1979; Ripsman, Taliaferro, & Lobell, 2016) or 'actorness' and 'sovereignty' (Berg & Kuusk, 2010; Smith, 2020).[2]

While these two dimensions – security and autonomy – may appear as more narrowly conceived than what the possibilities of hedging failure might involve (and states can lose territory and autonomy even if they are not hedging), they provide the needed organizing metric, allowing assessing hedging outcomes based on how much a specific hedging behaviour enhances the fundamental parameters of the hedging states' functioning as actors of international politics – physical survival/territorial sovereignty and state autonomy. Empirically, state autonomy can be measured by any changes in the state's capacity to behave actively and deliberately in relation to other actors in the international system and pursue strategies it sees fit to secure its survival independently and without

---

[2] According to the realist tradition, security has been seen as the most fundamental objective of any state so as other goals, such as economic development or social wellbeing, can hardly be achieved without security (Morgenthau, 1948; Waltz, 1979; Mearsheimer, 2001).

external coercion to change them. Territorial integrity can be measured by changes in the size of the state's territory. Hedging is successful if it can prevent the loss of territory and autonomy – when there are no observable changes or gains in the state's territorial sovereignty and capacity to act independently. It fails if it results in a loss of autonomy – in the form of greater dependence on external security provider(s) or (re)alignment with one great power at the costs of positive relations with the other – or territory – when armed aggression results in the occupation of territory and/or territorial incursions and encroachments.

In reality, the losses of territorial sovereignty and autonomy are not always absolute but relative: even a strong security dependence allows some degree of autonomy, and territorial occupation often leads to lasting territorial disputes rather than clear-cut losses or gains of territory. Therefore, hedging is most likely to be partially successful, meaning it helps mitigate the damaging impact of external forces on state security and may entail states sacrificing one component of security for the other, for example, relinquishing their autonomy to ensure physical survival and, in a less likely scenario, making territorial concessions to retain autonomy.[3] A few recent studies of hedging describe how some Asia-Pacific hedging states, such as Vietnam, the Philippines, Malaysia, Thailand, and New Zealand, having recognized the growing security challenges of their changing strategic environments, started to sacrifice their strategic autonomy and diversity of contacts for closer security ties with or accommodation of one of the competing great powers, the US or China. Such a transition has made their hedging profiles resemble more one-sided alignment behaviours, such as balancing and bandwagoning (Suzuki & Lee, 2017, p. 129; Ciorciari, 2019, pp. 544–547; Korolev, 2019, pp. 438–443; Fortier & Massie, 2023; He & Feng, 2023, p. 2), which is not costless in terms of strategic autonomy but arguably less harmful to their overall security under the circumstances. As the analysis in Section 4 demonstrates, the case of the Philippines represents such a trade-off, resulting in only partial hedging success. In contrast, the cases of Malaysia and Vietnam, on the one hand, and Georgia and Ukraine, on the other, are relatively more straightforward cases of hedging success and failure based on the criteria of security and autonomy.

Further analysis of the existing hedging literature reveals the importance of three key variables affecting hedging outcomes: *structural uncertainty*, the *availability of protective options*, and decision-makers' *geopolitical prudence*.

---

[3] For a more complex trade-offs between aspects of sovereignty and autonomy faced by states, see Krasner (1999). For examples of some Asia-Pacific hedging states compromising their autonomy for closer security ties with great powers, see Suzuki & Lee (2017), Ciorciari (2019), Korolev (2019), and Fortier & Massie (2023).

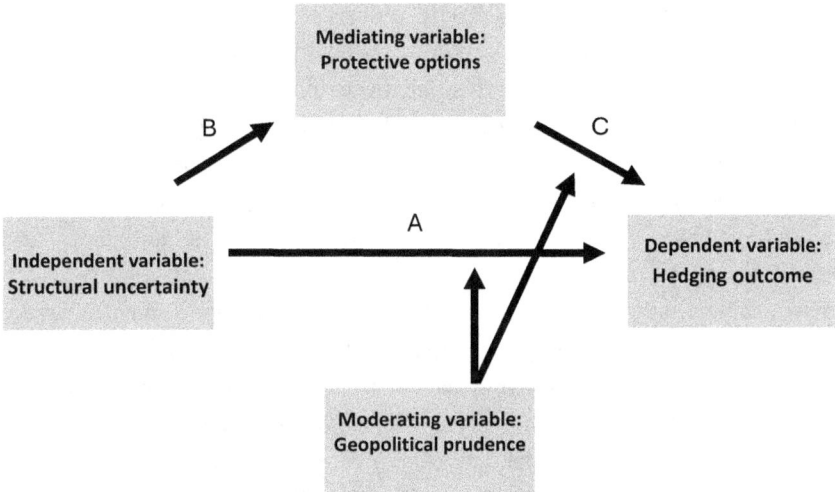

Figure 1 The theoretical model of hedging effectiveness

The relationship between these variables forms a model of hedging (Figure 1) in which changes in and between the variables affect hedging outcomes. Each variable and the pattern of interaction between them in generating causal impact require further specification.

2.1 Structural Uncertainty

At the international-systemic level, hedging is premised on *structural uncertainty* (Goh, 2006; Jackson, 2014; Ciorciari, 2019; Haacke, 2019; Korolev, 2019; Lai & Kuik, 2020; Smith, 2020) – the first (independent) variable in our model. Smaller states have stronger incentives to hedge when uncertainty about the state of great power competition is high, and policymakers are 'uncertain' about the directions and outcomes of the international order transition (He & Feng, 2023, p. 15). Hedging works in the face of uncertainty, whereas certainty over great powers' capabilities and intentions is believed to lead to clearer alignments (Haacke, 2019, pp. 393–394). Dealing with uncertainty is the goal of hedging.

Hedging literature defines uncertainty vaguely as a condition related to the nature of the international environment after the end of the Cold War bipolarity (Ciorciari, 2019; Korolev, 2019, p. 423). Uncertainty appears to overlap with other terms describing the intensity of great power competition, such as, for example, 'permissiveness' of the regional geopolitical environment, which Smith (2020, pp. 590–592) considers to be inversely related to the level of enmity between great powers and the initial key factor hedging states must consider. Similarly, Tessman (2012) talks about a 'deconcentrating international environment' under which second-tier states tend to adopt hedging strategies; during the 'concentrated' structures, bandwagoning is a better strategy. This conceptualization resembles Beeson and Higgott's (2014, pp. 224–225) notion of 'hegemonic decompression', under which smaller powers can better exercise their agency. According to Fortier and Massie (2023, p. 5), second-tier states can only hedge when they perceive the balance of power as 'ambiguous' and neither the rising nor declining great power as an imminent security threat. These characteristics make the international environment open-ended and more 'uncertain'. Korolev (2019, p. 425) defines structural uncertainty in terms of great power confrontation, arguing that when such confrontation intensifies, the structural uncertainty decreases, and smaller states start experiencing increasing difficulties with both equidistancing from great powers and pursuing counteracting policies that constitute hedging. Ripsman, Taliaferro, and Lobell (2016, pp. 45–57) talk about 'clarity' of systemic imperatives as a key dimension of the system that pertains to the scope of information that the system provides and reflects 'clarity of signals and information the international system presents to states'. High clarity, in turn, is characterized by 'clear threats' – states that display revisionism or hostility to harm other states' territorial integrity or core interests, possess the capabilities to do so, and carry a sense of imminence that they will use those capabilities to inflict harm (Ripsman, Taliaferro, and Lobell, 2016, p. 46).[4] This, in turn, links the discussion to the concept of the 'threat environment', which also implies identifying potential adversaries and assessing their military capabilities and intentions (Stein, 2013; Tu et al., 2024).

Drawing on the above conceptual analysis, this study defines structural uncertainty by two interrelated components: great powers' *capabilities*, which determine power structure in a region, and *intentions*, captured through the great powers' actual balancing behaviour against each other, which determines the level of pressure on smaller powers in the same region. The two are related because balancing intentions materialize, and balancing becomes more feasible, after accumulating sufficient capabilities. The first indicator (capabilities) concerns the structural power distribution and is operationalized through the most widely used, even though considered crude, indicators of national power – Gross National Product (GNP) and annual defence spending. It can be argued that the idea that uncertainty affects hedging outcomes is less intuitive when it comes to the capabilities (compared to intentions) due to the seemingly straightforward nature of this indicator. However, in the real world, state capabilities

---

[4] While emphasizing the usefulness of their concept of clarity, Ripsman, Taliaferro, and Lobell (2016, p. 51) admit that it is not a 'precise formula' but an early conceptual guideline that needs further elaboration.

can be less certain than they might seem. Nor is it always certain what specific states are capable of when having a given level of material capabilities. As the case of Georgia in Section 3 demonstrates, despite Russia's massive military modernization programs in the early 2000s and its more-than-obvious power preponderance vis-à-vis Georgia in 2008, authorities in Tbilisi believed that Russia remained backward militarily and, therefore, would not dare to invade the way it did. Even during the Cold War, when there should have been no uncertainty about the US and Soviet capabilities, analysts document a dramatic divergence in and controversy over the Western estimates of the trends in Soviet defence spending and defence policy (Noren, 1995), suggesting that some estimates, used in US successive presidential administrations for official purposes, tended to be significantly biased, contributing to US foreign policy decisions that were not in the nation's best interests (Holzman, 1989). These examples show that the perceptions of the structure of international politics at a given time matter, and the information derived from the seemingly obvious basic indicators of state capabilities (GDP and military spending) may not be accurate and reliable and may, at best, indicate the direction of the structural change, thus highlighting the need for geopolitical prudence – our model's third variable.

The second, behavioural indicator of structural uncertainty (intentions) is captured through Buzan and Wæver's (2003) idea of geopolitically charged Regional Security Complexes (RSC), which helps assess the regional intensity of great power balancing and connects the global power structure with regional security patterns, in which smaller states will usually find themselves locked into an RSC with their neighbours. As they consolidate, such RSCs become contentious, great-power-dominated regional settings of security interdependence where states' security concerns become intertwined so that actions by one member of the complex inevitably reverberate in others' security considerations. Within the most geopolitically charged RSCs, the states' security cannot be considered separate from each other (Buzan & Wæver, 2003, p. 46). Competing great powers involved in an RSC formation try to prevail in their peer competition. They intrude into each other's areas of strategic interests, making the geopolitical environment less permissive and pressuring RSC's smaller members to take sides. The geopolitical environment becomes less permissive, and uncertainty declines, reducing the wiggle room for smaller powers to hedge. To further operationalize an RSC's intensity, this study draws on Götz's (2019) suggestion that the level of external pressure on a country [and, hence, uncertainty] is a function of the security relationship between the actual or potential rivals of that country and states or territories in its immediate vicinity. External pressure increases [and uncertainty decreases] when a rival great power displays willingness to engage smaller powers surrounding the other great power in substantive military cooperation, such as troops deployment or defence agreements, or increase its presence in that power's area of priority strategic interests (Götz, 2019, p. 5).

The RSC theory is useful in the context of this study because it provides a conceptual lens for gauging the change of structural uncertainty levels in a region through its idea of the varying intensity of great power 'penetration' of an RSC, thus helping demonstrate the variation of the model's independent variable. RSCs are substructures/subsets of the international system, embedded in the global polarity and affected by the global-level great power security dynamics (Buzan & Wæver, 2003, pp. 45–51). As such, they are expected to be penetrated by the great powers that, projecting their influences and rivalries into the rest of the system, are drawn into a region along the lines of rivalry existing within it (Buzan & Wæver, 2003, p. 52). Thus, RSCs can be extensively penetrated by global powers' interests, in which case regional rivalry patterns will align with the global powers' ones. Alternatively, they can be less penetrated, in which case the regional dynamics will have a substantial degree of autonomy from the patterns set by the great powers. Depending on the degree of great power penetration, RSCs can evolve from the regular ones, characterized by minimal great power penetration, to the great power-dominated or heavily penetrated ones, in which regional or global great power interests significantly affect the RSC's internal dynamics, to, eventually, 'overlays' – conditions when great power interests come to dominate a region so heavily that any local patterns of security relations virtually ceases to operate (Buzan & Wæver, 2003, pp. 61–62).[5] This process of RSC intensification reflects the decline of structural uncertainty from high to zero.[6]

Informed by this conceptualization, the structural uncertainty environment for the Southeast Asian cases (the Philippines, Malaysia, and Vietnam) is assessed through the analysis of an RSC formation in the Indo-Pacific involving the US and China, whereas that for the post-Soviet cases (Georgia and Ukraine) is assessed through the RSC involving Russia, on the one hand, and the EU and the US, on the other. This study, thus, looks at two RSCs: an Indo-Pacific RSC, increasingly penetrated by the dynamics of US–China rivalry; and the post-Soviet RSC, defined by the competition for influence between Russia and the EU/US. The two RSCs are treated separately because, while the US has

---

[5] According to Buzan and Wæver (2003, 61–62), examples of overlay are European colonisation of Asia, Africa, and the Americas, and the situation in Europe during the Cold War, when the European security dynamic was overlaid by the USA-USSR superpower rivalry.
[6] Movements in both directions are possible as, according to Buzan and Wæver (2003, 64), 'in practice it will often be a former and future RSC that is overlaid'.

significant entanglements in both regions (and operates at both the global and regional levels), the polarity in both regions is defined by competition with different powers, which makes them mutually exclusive to a significant extent. China's interests and the dynamics of its system-level competition with the US do not heavily penetrate the geopolitical milieu around either Ukraine or Georgia, while Russia–EU and Russia–US rivalries do. Similarly, Russia's role in the Indo-Pacific RSC is insignificant compared to that of the US and China. These patterns generate two sufficiently distinct sets of regional security interdependencies, especially from the standpoint of the smaller powers in focus, to differentiate the two RSCs. Simultaneously, regarding the Southeast Asian cases explored in Section 4, it is possible to talk about the South China Sea 'subcomplex', embedded in the larger Indo-Pacific RSC, or, alternatively, the Indo-Pacific RSC can be presented as a wider 'supercomplex' of which the South China Sea RSC is a part, along with, for example, the Taiwan Strait RSC. These definitional variations do not change the idea of an interconnected and increasingly geopolitically charged regional environment in which the three Southeast Asian states reside, but recognize some variety in security interconnectedness across a wider regional pattern.

At the same time, while the great power rivalry increasingly penetrated and affected the two regions over the period covered in this study, resulting in dropping levels of uncertainty, both RSCs fell short of an overlay completely defined by great power rivalry and characterized by zero levels of structural uncertainty.[7] In Southeast Asia, Malaysia, Vietnam, the Philippines, and other states continue to possess significant agency and actorness to play an important role in the regional security dynamics and how the regional security agenda is defined and framed (e.g., through ASEAN), making the interests *within* the region more pronounced. The more contingent, exposed, and difficult geopolitical environment of Georgia and Ukraine is still defined by the actors *in* the region (including Russia and the EU, with the latter not always being on the same page with the US) in a way that brings the pressures of local geographical proximities to the fore and shapes the main security dynamics of the region; Ukraine's hedging prior to the war itself has brought regional specifics to the game. It is, therefore, more accurate to characterize the two RSCs as becoming heavily penetrated (with the degree of penetration

---

[7] It can be argued that after Russia invaded Ukraine in February 2022, or even earlier, the post-Soviet RSC became overlaid. This might be the case to an extent, but, on the other hand, the continued strong regional dynamics, the growing complexity of Russia's relations with other post-Soviet states (including Georgia), and Russia's overall limited military presence across the region, compared to the years of the Cold War, would make one take issue with this assumption.

increasing over the last two decades or so) but not overlaid because their regional-level dynamic remain significant.[8]

Understood this way, structural uncertainty is a variable rather than a constant. As some argued, different states face different degrees of complexity and uncertainty, and the clarity of each state's external environment varies across time and space, revealing different amounts of information about strategic constraints and opportunities (Goldman, 2011, p. 140). External pressure is a 'continuum' (Götz, 2019, p. 102), and strategic environments can be permissive and restrictive depending on the imminence and magnitude of threats and opportunities (Ripsman, Taliaferro, & Lobell, 2016, p. 53). Therefore, different geopolitical environments are either more or less certain, or relatively uncertain, depending on the degree and intensiveness of great power rivalry, with the war or imminent conflict posing an immediate threat to states' survival and autonomy having the highest certainty (as in overlays). It is, thus, more accurate to talk about the *level* of uncertainty and its impact on the likelihood of hedging success or failure. While it does not dictate the specific behaviour of states, it generates dispositional pressures that frame the overall thrust of hedging behaviour, affecting the variance in hedging states' choices of tools, tactics, and policies. In this study, uncertainty is higher when great powers' capabilities are unknown or unclear (or not accurately read), and the relevant RSC does not clearly signal a high intensity of great power balancing because great powers do not increasingly engage smaller powers in each other's area of priority strategic interests in substantive military cooperation. The level of uncertainty is lower when capabilities are clear and allow balancing, and the RSC indicates great powers' strong intentions to balance.

2.2 The Availability of Protective Options

The second variable affecting hedging outcomes is the availability of a *protective option*. According to Ciorciari (2019, p. 546), for Southeast Asian states to hedge effectively, a credible US security commitment is needed; otherwise, there will be little choice but to accommodate Beijing. Similarly, Smith (2020) highlights that smaller states hedge more comfortably with an

---

[8] In pursuit of definitional precision, it is also important not to lose the forest for the trees. As Buzan and Wæver themselves admit (2003, 63), there are problems with determining the boundaries between the concepts of overlay an mere heavy penetration of and RSC by great powers, as well as between complexes, subcomplexes, and supercomplexes, which 'like most things in social science are matters of definition and degree rather than sharp lines of discontinuity'. In the present research, the theoretical discussion of the RSC evolution is intended to help flesh out the variation of the independent variable – the level of structural uncertainty – in the two regions of interest. Moreover, in the real world, policy practitioners' situational actions and interpretations will add a twist on how regional systems are defined.

agreed regional security architecture that can mitigate external threats, if not prevent great power aggressive behaviour. The availability of a protective option reflects the possibility for smaller powers to turn to external defence partner(s) for protection in time of need and is related more to regional geopolitics than the international structure.

The availability of a protective option enters the model as a mediator variable – it mediates the causal impact of the independent variable (structural uncertainty) on the dependent variable (hedging), or, in other words, structural uncertainty affects hedging outcomes through the protective option variable. Specifically, when structural uncertainty drops and great power rivalry intensifies, the availability of a protective option becomes critical (but simultaneously surrounded by growing strategic complexity that smaller states must deal with), which incentivises smaller states' cultivation of protective options as a hedge against the worst-case scenario (causal pathway B on Figure 1). In turn, the availability of such options has direct implications for hedging outcomes because it can help mitigate or reverse such a scenario (pathway C). In other words, the protective option variable serves to illustrate important aspects of the causal relationship between the independent and dependent variables. This idea can be traced in some literature on hedging. For example, Ciorciari (2019, p. 525) talks about hedging *as* the development of protective options that smaller powers' governments can activate if security conditions worsen. Cultivation of protective options by pursuing security cooperations and diplomatic ententes is, therefore, 'embedded' in smaller powers' hedging strategies (Ciorciari, 2019, pp. 541–545). Similarly, various scholars have analogized hedging with the cultivation of a form of 'insurance' as a way to set up a fallback protection option if the external threat comes to pass (Lake, 1996; Foot, 2006; Medeiros, 2005; Tessman & Wolfe, 2011). Cultivating too little protection (or 'insurance') through hedging results in the insufficiency or absence of adequate protective measures when the security environment deteriorates and can leave smaller states exposed to intensifying external threats, increasing the chances of hedging failure.

Protective options do not need to be alliances and can take the form of flexible alignments without rigid formal agreements delineated by behavioural actions, as long as there is an indication of the commitment to protect in time of need. The general appeal of these more flexible limited alignments is that they can help address smaller powers' security risks without becoming inevitably embroiled in great power hard balancing, which leaves cooperation opportunities with the competing great powers open (Goh, 2005; Kuik, 2008; Tessman & Wolfe, 2011). Smaller states can also hedge against security risks by cultivating multilateral protective options, which can include organizations and third countries not directly involved in the RSC but that can provide means to mitigate possible aggression by competing major powers. The cases of Malaysia and Vietnam demonstrate how hedging states can use regional institutions and reach out to other extra-regional great powers to cultivate protective options. Empirically, the availability of a protective option can be captured as credible self-help capabilities (which is unlikely for smaller powers) or the availability of unwavering commitment from a larger defence partner or a security institution to provide political and military support commensurate to the smaller power's needs in the time of crisis and the level of the great power's reassurances before the crisis.

At the same time, being an ally of a competing great power does not automatically cancel hedging as long as the great power relationship falls short of open confrontation. South Korea, Japan, Australia, Canada, and other explicitly aligned states have been studied as hedging cases in the literature (Chan, 2019; Koga, 2018; Kuik, 2021, pp. 8–9; Fortier & Massie, 2023; He & Feng, 2023). However, whether a cultivated protective option is an alliance based on a tight security pact or not should have implications for hedging outcomes in terms of the security-autonomy trade-off. Tighter alliances generally entail explicit defence commitment, extensive joint exercises, and other institutional attributes conducive to strong defence cooperation. In these cases, under declining uncertainty, smaller states can either switch, voluntarily or not, to balancing or bandwagoning, depending on their pre-existing alliance relationship, thus pre-emptively edging hedging behaviour, as did Australia and Canada (Fortier & Massie, 2023; He & Feng, 2023). It is even more so if one or both rivalling great powers are the only actors for possible protection, in which case they will expect and compel their smaller allies to do more for the alliance to facilitate balancing. In return, the great power will ramp up its security guarantees, further tightening the alliance with the small power. Doing so, however, can render the smaller state highly dependent on its protector and undermine the government's autonomy while displaying hostility toward a potential rival, limiting the available policy options. In these cases, it is, therefore, possible to talk about a hedging failure as a loss of autonomy more than territorial sovereignty.

Whether the protective option is in the form of a flexible alignment, a multilateral arrangement, or a conventional alliance, its availability and activation under the conditions of intensifying great power rivalry are not always straightforward; even in rock-solid alliances, the dangers of abandonment or inadequate assistance exist (Snyder, 1984). This is illustrated by the case of the Philippines in Section 4, when the Philippines' President Rodrigo Duterte, obviously knowing that the US is Manila's treaty ally, was not confident in the

US's commitment to defend the Philippines in case of direct military confrontation with Beijing. Thus, as structural uncertainty about intensifying US–China rivalry declined and Manila's relations with Beijing deteriorated, resulting in a greater need for protection, Duterte worked on re-cultivating the protective option by utilizing a hedging strategy. Once Washington re-confirmed its commitment to the security alliance with the Philippines and strengthened the bilateral security cooperation, thus activating the protective measures, the Philippines switched from hedging to a balancing posture against China. Things become trickier when the protective options available to smaller states are in the form of an informal alignment without rigid security commitments. In this case, the availability of the protective option is ambiguous, and smaller states' governments are in danger of believing there is access to protection in times of need when, in fact, there is no such access.

2.3 Geopolitical Prudence

The challenge of assessing structural uncertainty and the availability of protective options brings us to the third variable – decision-makers' *geopolitical prudence*. A few studies have alluded to the importance of prudence for hedging. Generally, hedging requires a 'sensible' strategic response to uncertainty (Ciorciari, 2019, p. 526). Kuik (2021, pp. 3, 7) associates hedging with an 'instinctive behaviour' and a 'survival instinct', highlighting policymakers' capacity to anticipate threats and avoid dangers. Smith (2020, p. 591) characterizes smaller states' perceptions as 'giving value' to systemic changes and affecting the assessments of the regional geopolitical environment. Ciorciari and Haacke (2019, p. 372) also see hedging as a 'prudent form of behaviour' that relies on adequate risk assessments. Wilkins (2021, p. 9) talks about 'manual hedging', highlighting the role of policymakers' capacity to steer hedging based on their assessment of risks and threats. Jones and Jenne (2021, p. 3) highlight the importance of a 'pragmatic understanding' of international politics and present hedging as 'a counsel of prudence' that must fit strategic ends to limited means without ignoring specific situations that affect policy deliberation. Quoting Aristotle's *Rhetoric*, they argue that the wisdom of prudence is meant to 'determine not ends but means to ends, that is what is most useful to do' (Jones & Jenne, 2021, p. 18). In other words, hedging requires self-awareness, restraint, and the capacity to do 'not what is beautiful to say but what is necessary in practice' – pragmatic, not dogmatic, things (Jones & Jenne, 2021, pp. 15–26).

Geopolitical prudence is hard to operationalize and is an inevitably imperfect name for policymakers' capacity to assess and manage external risks and threats in each geopolitical environment to avoid falling victim to great power rivalry (Ciorciari, 2019; Haacke, 2019; Lai & Kuik, 2020; Smith, 2020). It includes carefully evaluating the international system, key players' national interests, and leaders' assessments of risks and opportunities in their nation's relations with the potential hedging target (Gerstl, 2022, pp. 4, 23). The practice of prudence, thus, can be seen as situational. It is meant to help smaller states confronted by great power rivalry achieve a practical and context-specific understanding of international politics that emphasises contingency, historical example, immediate facts and specific situations, as well as adjustment to international events and agendas, and is informed by calmness of mind as the antidote to zealotry, passion, and enthusiasm (Jones & Jenne, 2021, p. 18).

Therefore, prudence is operationalized in connection to the other two causal variables in the model – as decision-makers' capacity to make prudent judgements about the level of structural uncertainty (i.e., capabilities and behaviour of the great powers within the same RSC) and the availability of protective options, and modify their hedging behaviour in the context of a specific case. Specifically, to avoid hedging failure, smaller states' policymakers need to accurately assess the distribution of power and the intensity of balancing between the key competing great powers within the RSC, as well as their partners' security commitments, to avoid a situation where they believe there is a protective option when, in fact, there is none. This makes prudence a moderating variable that affects the strength of the relationships between the independent and dependent variables (path A) and between the mediator and dependent variables (path C in Figure 1).

Defined in this way, the conception of prudence requires further specification. Drawing on the philosophical works of Edmund Burke, Confucius, and Machiavelli, Jones and Jenne (2021, p. 20) discern 'active' and 'reactive' prudence. Active prudence entails a clear willingness to take greater risks to explore possibilities open to action, whereas reactive prudence focuses on modest goals, including limited order, peace, and accommodation (Jones & Jenne, 2021, p. 20). At the same time, the less risky reactive prudence is characterized by 'scepticism toward any radical transformation of the world' (Jones & Jenne, 2021, p. 20). It is this reactive prudence that is believed to be the most important, but often neglected, tool for hedging that should inform smaller powers' behaviour (Jones & Jenne, 2021, p. 25). It is identifiable in some Southeast Asian states' approaches to diplomacy. For example, Lee Kuan Yew of Singapore emphasized 'pragmatism' or 'practical reasoning', based on restraint and checking excess, which must be the central principle guiding smaller Southeast Asian states' behaviour amid intensifying US–China rivalry (Mahbubani, 2017).

This discussion of the more risk-averse (reactive) vis-à-vis more daring (active) prudence dovetails well with the risk-mitigation versus gains-maximization logics of hedging distinguishable in the literature; hedging appears as a form of behaviour beset with a trade-off between these two hedging goals. According to Gerstl (2022, p. 113), states hedge to minimize security risks *and* maximize economic benefits.[9] Tunsjø (2013, pp. 26–27) suggests that hedging combines shorts and longs and implies 'forgoing maximum possible profit to manage and minimise risk'. Ciorciari (2009, p. 168) views hedging as a strategy designed to optimize the 'risks and rewards' of security cooperation with great powers. Kuik (2008, 2016) argues that hedging can mitigate risks and maximise benefits, suggesting that a hedging state can pursue 'risk-contingency' and 'returns-maximizing' policy options. Smith's (2018, p. 10) conceptualization breaks down hedging into a low-cost–low-reward cautious/modest hedging, which signals ambiguity and creates levels of uncertainty amongst the targets of the hedge, and a high-cost–high-reward brazen/assertive hedging when the state manoeuvres to achieve the outcomes it desires. Continuing this logic, Gerst (2022, pp. 112–113) further suggests that hedging can have negative incentives of avoiding an alignment (or being forced to align) with a great power and positive incentives, such as reaping political, economic, or security benefits from all great powers.

Indeed, smaller states' leaders and ruling elites can aim for different levels of risk mitigation: some can be more risk-averse, while others may have a greater appetite for gain, trying to maximize the fruits of engagement (Ciorciari, 2019; Jones & Jenne, 2021). This orientation affects the accuracy of governments' assessment of potential threats and choice of adequate hedging mechanisms. Like in financial markets where gain-seeking investors suffer major losses, gain-maximizing leaders of smaller powers are more prone to risk miscalculation, leaving their states more vulnerable to external predation (Ciorciari, 2019). As demonstrated in the following, it is even more so when great power rivalry within an RSC intensifies and pressure on smaller powers grows, resulting in the two logics of hedging (risk-mitigation and gains-maximization) starting to contradict each other and work at cross purposes. Prudence can thus be understood in terms of risk-mitigation versus gains-maximization under declining structural uncertainty.

---

[9] The debate about whether hedging should do with military strategy only (Lim & Cooper, 2015) or go beyond that (López i Vidal & Pelegrín, 2018) is a different matter that has not been resolved. This paper believes that the general principles of maximising gains and minimising risks apply to hedging in any sphere. It also subscribes to the point that as great power rivalry intensifies and systemic pressure increases, it is increasingly difficult to demarcate security from economic or political engagements (Korolev, 2019).

Therefore, in the context of our theoretical model, prudence has to do with *how* smaller states' governments assess structural uncertainty and protective options and adjust their behaviour. Regarding structural uncertainty, a more prudent risk-mitigating approach will differ from the less prudent gains-maximizing approach in terms of the smaller powers' conception of their agency and actorness in the context of intensifying great power rivalry. More specifically, a risk-mitigating approach would require smaller powers' acute awareness of the limits of their agency, demonstrated through explicit acknowledgements of limited self-help capabilities and great power rivalry being a 'given' exogenous factor that smaller states cannot significantly change. Thus, prudent leaders would hedge their own bets only, trying to avoid sensitive issue areas that are objects of great power rivalry (i.e., great powers' economic and security stakes in a region), displaying reluctance to elevate specific areas of disagreement (e.g., a territorial disputes or other disagreements with larger powers that are not by default the object of great power rivalry) to the level of systemic great power competition because doing so, while might promise larger gains, is more likely to embroil the hedging smaller powers into great power confrontation.[10] Prudent smaller states would proactively reach out to extra-regional powers or organizations to diversify strategic links and foster a multipolar environment, which extends the room for hedging.

In contrast, the less prudent gains-maximizing approach to assessing structural uncertainty would entail enacting an idealized conception of actorness, in which smaller states aim to change great power behaviour or transform the trajectory of great power politics in their favour, underestimating the risks.[11] In this case, the scope of smaller power hedging would trespass into the economic and security stakes of the competing great powers and indicate a willingness to link specific regional issues in a relationship with a great power, which are not an object of systemic great power rivalry, to competition between the great powers. This would also involve a more brazen back and forth between the competing great powers and weaker attempts to reach out to extra-regional actors to diversify the stakes. When structural uncertainty declines, such an approach is more likely to lock smaller powers into an irreconcilably

---

[10] The Philippines' embarking, together with the US, on the policy of 'lawfare' against China's maritime claims and thus shifting the crux of the SCS dispute with China from sovereignty over isles and islands to the systemic China–US competition, which triggered China's retaliation against the Philippines, illustrates this point.

[11] These differences become clear when comparing Ukraine under Yanukovych with Malaysia during the same period of time. While Malaysia's leaders tried to minimise risks by displaying acute awareness of the limits of their agency, Yanukovych became a case of idealised agency and capacity to navigate Russia-West rivalry that resulted in disregarding the stark power imbalances in Eastern Europe.

binary – either one great power or the other – geopolitical configuration, making them more exposed to great powers' competing interests.

Regarding the availability of a protective option, a more prudent risk-mitigating approach differs from the less prudent gains-maximizing approach in terms of different degrees of security commitments from their larger partners or security organizations that smaller hedging states will deem acceptable when they hedge. Smaller powers adopting a more brazen gains-maximizing approach to hedging appear more willing to be involved in complex issues of great power rivalry without clear security commitments from either one of the competing great powers or organizations and/or third parties/countries that are not directly involved in the great power rivalry. In contrast, the risk-mitigating approach would require hedging smaller powers to seek unwavering confirmation of a commitment from a larger defence partner or a security institution to provide political and military support in a time of crisis.

If a government is prudent, it is most likely to be prudent in its assessments of both structural uncertainty and protective option, in which case hedging is least likely to fail even in a heavily penetrated RSC, unless the great power rivalry develops into an open confrontation, turning the RSC into an overlay. However, some variations, such as when smaller powers' leaders are more prudent in assessing the protective option than structural uncertainty, or vice versa, depending on the circumstances, cannot be ruled out. While these variations can have implications for the hedging outcomes, such uneven or partial prudence will still help reduce the likelihood of unequivocal hedging failure (the loss of both security and autonomy). A prudent risk-mitigating approach to structural uncertainty helps expand hedging opportunities, thus minimizing, or at least delaying, the need to activate the protective option, making the accurate assessment of it less critical, even though not unimportant; at the same time, it can buy time to clarify and confirm the availability of protection and modify behaviour accordingly. Similarly, while prudence towards the availability of the protective option may not revert great power rivalry, it can help prevent a situation when a smaller state confronts a great power without security guarantees.

The last point about the theoretical model that requires mentioning is the dynamic nature of interaction between the three causal variables: the level of structural uncertainty affects the role of the other two variables (protective option and geopolitical prudence). The idea of 'interaction' between causal variables of different levels of analysis in international relations can be traced in neoclassical realist theoretical models, where systemic (independent) variables affect the scope of the role of the unit-level (intervening) variables. While neoclassical realism does not specify how exactly particular intervening state-level variables are influenced by the independent variable, it contains the idea that the role of state-level factors changes depending on the intensity of systemic pressure, which is relevant to our discussion. Ripsman, Taliaferro, and Lobell (2016, pp. 93, 146) highlight that a state's response to external threats is determined by an interaction between the external environment and unit-level factors in which 'not only should the IVVs [intervening variables] interact with the DVs [dependent variables] . . ., but the intervening variables themselves can also be influenced by . . . independent variables (IVs)'. Thus, in a highly restrictive strategic environment, characterized by apparent systemic imperatives, international-level factors will have a greater impact on states' foreign policy. In contrast, in a less restrictive environment with unclear systemic imperatives, there is more room for unit-level factors to play a causal role. The impact of domestic-level forces on foreign policymaking is a function of the relative permissiveness of a state's strategic environment coupled with the clarity of systemic imperative (Ripsman, 2009, pp. 186–187; Götz, 2021, p. 8). Fordham's (2012, p. 270) analysis of the interaction of international political environments and domestic interests in the US context also suggests that 'the effects of domestic and international variables depend on one another'. International considerations enter the model 'interactively with the domestic political process determining the interests of the faction that happens to control the state' (Fordham, 2012, p. 255). Unit-level factors are also believed to condition whether states can react to international stimuli promptly and effectively (Götz, 2021, p. 4).

While the nature of the system-unit interaction in foreign policy formation remains a source of confusion within the neoclassical realist literature (Götz, 2021, p. 2),[12] the above insights into interactions between causal variables of different levels inform our conceptualization of the relationship between our three variables in generating impact on hedging outcomes. As previously mentioned, the degree of structural uncertainty affects the likelihood of hedging success or failure. It makes hedging easier or more difficult, but does not independently determine the outcome. High structural uncertainty is associated with low systemic pressure on smaller states and high systemic permissiveness. The system is rarefied/decompressed. Hedging becomes easy, the need for access to protective options less urgent, and the costs of mistakes lower, reducing the need for geopolitical prudence and allowing for some degree of imprudence (in the form of idealized self-agency and willingness to take risks without firm security guarantees). As the structural uncertainty level drops from high to low and balancing dynamics between great powers becomes more

---

[12] Neoclassical realism is a broad and debated school. For a vivid debate about whether neoclassical realism qualifies and should be maintained as a coherent theoretical school, see Narizny (2017) and the related correspondence by experts in the field Fiammenghi et al. (2018).

pronounced, systemic pressure on smaller powers intensifies, the room for strategic manoeuvre shrinks, and smaller powers become pressed to take sides in great power competition. As this process unfolds, the risks of conflict grow, as does the need for access to protective options and demands on policymakers' prudence. But now, access to a protective option is surrounded by greater strategic complexity that smaller states must navigate. The costs of misjudgements about structural uncertainty and the availability of protective options soar, making policymakers' geopolitical prudence critical.

3 Structure, Protective Options, and Geopolitical (Im)Prudence: Georgia and Ukraine

The 2008 Russia-Georgia war and the 2014 Ukraine crisis, which harmfully ended Tbilisi's and Kyiv's hedging, happened under declining structural uncertainty as the post-Soviet RSC gradually became heavily penetrated. Regarding the first indicator (relative capabilities), Russia's place in the structural power distribution has changed significantly since the 1990s. Despite often being pictured as a declining power, Russia's GNP increased 11-fold from a $196 billion post-Soviet low in 1999 to $2.292 trillion in 2013, before the Ukraine crisis (World Bank, 2019). Changes in annual military spending further demonstrated the change. With all the caveats related to the fluctuation of Russia's local currency exchange rates, during the decade before the Ukraine Crisis (between 2003 and 2014), Russia's military spending grew by 108 per cent (Perlo-Freeman & Solmirano, 2014, p. 2).

At the same time, market exchange rate calculations underestimate the real volume of spending in countries with relatively small per-capita incomes, such as Russia and China. In this regard, Kofman and Conolly (2019) ask: how can Russia, with its defence spending allegedly on par with France and the United Kingdom, maintain over a million military personnel and carry out procurements of cutting-edge military hardware that dwarf that of most European powers combined? Most of the available data ignores dramatic fluctuations of local currency exchange rates, such as the sharp depreciation of the Russian ruble in 2014–2015, when in dollar value the Russian military expenditure was reported as declining, but it increased significantly in ruble terms. Moreover, Russia produces most of its weaponry and does not import costly arms from overseas, meaning that a ruble spent at home buys significantly more than a dollar spent abroad (Kofman and Connolly, 2019).[13] The purchasing power

---

[13] This observation further illustrates the point that such a seemingly straightforward indicator as the volume of military spending may be hard to pin down empirically and put into a comparative context, which creates some uncertainty around Russia's (or any other country with sizable grey economy) actual military capabilities.

parity (PPP)-adjusted estimates of military budgets allow measuring non-traded goods and services that dominate military expenditure in Russia and show that Russia's military budget in 2019 reached $166 billion (Wezeman, 2020), which is believed to be a conservative figure that excludes hidden military expenditures that exist in Russia. As a result of large-scale rearmament programs based on these growing material capabilities, Russia has become more resurgent and is aspiring to restore its spheres of influence.

In terms of the second indicator of structural uncertainty (intentions as indicated by the intensity of the relevant RSC), structural uncertainty has also dwindled dramatically as a highly contentious post-Soviet RSC gradually formed along the contact zone between the US/EU/NATO and Russia-led Eurasian Economic Union (EEU), aimed at re-establishing Russia's regional influence. This RSC became increasingly contentious and penetrated by great power rivalry as NATO was willing to engage smaller powers surrounding Russia in substantive military cooperation. The rounds of NATO eastward expansion, supported by the US, have traditionally been viewed by Moscow as a major security threat that requires a response. Moscow adopted a threatening approach towards smaller post-Soviet states and, after the Russia-Georgia war of 2008, started to seriously consider the possibility of military conflict with the West, marking a shift in its thinking about the future of warfare (Kashin, 2018, p. 217). Washington, in turn, started to identify Russia, together with China, as a threat and a major adversary (President of the United States, 2017, p. 25). At the same time, the analysis of Russia's approach to the post-Soviet space indicates the emergence of security interdependence – a situation when the RSC becomes more contentious because the security of one state cannot be considered separately from that of another. Thus, military conflicts with Georgia and Ukraine are viewed in Russia as necessary measures to deal with more significant external threats posed by the US and NATO (Sizov, 2009; Kashin, 2018). Through these conflicts, some experts with links to the Kremlin have argued, Russia gives 'a firm rebuff to the aggressors [NATO, backed by the US]' (Karaganov, 2011). Analysis of Russia's official documents also shows that 'major foreign powers' (the US) and their military-technical advancements, aimed at 'predominant superiority in the military sphere', pose an existential military threat (President of Russia, 2014). The region became heavily penetrated by competing great power interests, reducing the level of structural uncertainty.

While the gradual disappearance of structural uncertainty and the formation of contentious, heavily penetrated RSC in the region had varying permutations for Georgia and Ukraine, smaller states within the RSC became hard-pressed to navigate the intensifying great power rivalry and defend their national interests.

By the end of the 2000s, and clearly by the 2014 phase of the Ukraine crisis, the Russia-West competition for influence was intensifying, and the threat to smaller states posed by increasingly resurgent Russia was consolidating, with Moscow displaying clear intentions to use its power to realise its geopolitical ambitions. Georgia and Ukraine faced a starkly dangerous and heavily securitised regional environment, which raised demands on their leaders' geopolitical prudence to assess the structural pressures and availability of protective options.

3.1 Georgia: Declining Uncertainty and Imprudent Assessment of Protective Option

In the lead up to the Russia-Georgia war of August 2008, Georgian President Michael Saakashvili intensively cultivated ties with the US to reduce dependence on Moscow and create a protective option against potential Russian aggression. Georgia eagerly assumed the role of a 'beacon of liberty' in the Caucasus. It supported the most controversial aspects of US foreign policy by stationing more than 2,000 Georgian soldiers in Iraq, which made Georgia the third largest contingent in the coalition. It also signed a transit agreement allowing NATO to transport troops and equipment through Georgian air, sea, and land space (Cooley & Mitchell, 2009; Mouritzen & Wivel, 2012, p. 65).

The US reciprocated generously. It made Georgia its most important partner in the region and provided significant political, economic, and military aid, even after Saakashvili failed to live up to his promise of democratic reforms (Cooley & Mitchell, 2009, pp. 33–34; Mouritzen & Wivel, 2012, p. 107). Washington strongly supported Georgia's NATO membership, despite Russia's vehement resistance, and played a critical role in boosting Georgia's defence capabilities through military aid and training programs, such as the Georgia Train and Equip Program (2002–2004) and Sustainment and Stability Program (2005–2007). The ubiquitous presence of US advisors in the Georgian military, US-Georgia joint military exercises, unprecedented personal ties between the two governments, and Saakashvili's unparalleled access to the highest levels of the George Bush administration, along with bipartisan support that he had, signalled close alignment and boosted the Georgian leadership's confidence (Mouritzen & Wivel, 2012, pp. 98–99).

However, despite this seemingly obvious tilt towards the US, Saakashvili's behaviour was not unequivocal. Like other post-Soviet countries, Georgia could not leave post-Soviet Russia's sphere of influence and used hedging strategies to navigate the geopolitical complexities. While moving closer to the West, Saakashvili tried to advance relations with Russia, vowing to 'do everything' for that and stating that Georgia 'needs Russia as an ally, as a powerful partner'

(Saakashvili, 2004). Saakashvili was ready to work on signing a bilateral friendship treaty with Russia and wanted Moscow to help the Georgian government resume control over Abkhazia and South Ossetia (MacFarlane, 2016). He also emphasized that 'our main goal is the convergence of the American, Russian, and Georgian interests' (Osetinskii, 2004). His first official state visit was to Moscow, where he came 'to make friends' and assured that if Russia's peacekeepers withdrew from their bases, Georgia would not permit rights to any third country or take other steps that might undermine Russia's interests, to which Russia responded positively (Peuch, 2004). In April 2004, epitomizing his hedging approach, Saakashvili emphasized that the 'Russia or the West?' binary choice is problematic and infeasible and even made parallels between Russia and the US as possible guarantors of Georgia's territorial integrity.

Saakashvili's hedging was not in vain. Putin's National Security Council secretary, Igor Ivanov, facilitated the peaceful resignation and exit of Saakashvili's predecessor, Eduard Shevardnadze, after the Rose Revolution (MacFarlane, 2016). In May 2004, after Saakashvili visited Moscow, Russian and Georgian diplomats cooperated on the removal of Aslan Abashidze, the leader of the Adjarian local government, which helped to solve a political crisis in Georgia and restore Georgian government control over the Adjara autonomous region (Kakachia et al., 2013, pp. 80–90). The Russian foreign minister Sergei Lavrov even agreed to withdraw four Russian military bases from the Georgian territory that Russia was officially allowed to retain according to an agreement signed in 1995 (Sokov, 2005, pp. 2–4). In this context, Georgia's National Security Concept of 2005 ranked the presence of Russian military bases in Georgia as a low-security risk and did not perceive Russia as a serious military threat (Merabishvili & Kiss, 2016, p. 164).

These hedging initiatives started to crumble amid declining uncertainty around the intensifying US–Russia rivalry. The significant advancement of military cooperation with the US and the April 2008 Bucharest NATO summit's declaration that Georgia would inevitably join the alliance (NATO, 2008) consolidated Russia's perception of NATO as an imminent security threat. The demonstrable willingness of the US to engage Georgia in substantive military cooperation further intensified the hard balancing mentality in Moscow, making the geopolitical fault lines and the directions of US–Russia regional contestation more explicit. Immediately after the Bucharest summit, Russia published *The Russian President's Instructions to the Russian Federation Government with Regard to Abkhazia and South Ossetia* that pledged support for the two breakaway republics and stressed that Moscow would 'protect its citizens' (Putin, 2008). Russia also started arming separatists there (Asmus, 2010). Simultaneously, the US, well informed of the growing tensions, officially supported the Saakashvili administration's commitment to winning the two regions back (Mouritzen & Wivel, 2012, p. 98). Washington took the stance that this was a question of Georgia's territorial integrity, even though Georgia had governed neither of the two regions. Russians, in turn, on multiple occasions, have 'made it clear that they were not going to allow these regions [Abkhazia and South Ossetia] to be absorbed by Georgia, even under a federal formula' (Cooley & Mitchell, 2009, p. 32). The precipitating RSC increased demands on policymakers' prudence and the need for protective options.

However, the Georgian leadership appears to have misjudged both the level of structural uncertainty – by operating based on an inflated conception of its agency vis-à-vis Russia and US–Russia rivalry – and the availability of a protective option in the form of the United States – through its willingness to become involved in highly contentious issues of US–Russia rivalry without clear security commitments from either great power. It severely underestimated Russia's capabilities and intentions. Even though the US and its allies and their emboldening military support of Tbilisi might have contributed to this misperception (Mouritzen & Wivel, 2012, p. 110), evidence suggests that it is the Georgian leadership that displayed the lack of prudence. According to Nino Burjanadze, Speaker of the Georgian Parliament (9 November 2001– 7 June 2008) and acting President of Georgia (25 November 2007– 20 January 2008), Putin, in a direct conversation, warned Saakashvili that under no circumstances should he contemplate any military operation as long as Russian peacekeepers are stationed in Abkhazia and South Ossetia, 'otherwise the response will be rapid and fierce and may include military means' (Pozner, 2017). However, Burjanadze said, 'Saakashvili was somehow confident that Russia will not dare to interfere militarily into what the international community viewed as Georgia's domestic problem' (Pozner, 2017). Moreover, Saakashvili's immediate surroundings had people arguing that 'we have new tanks, but the Russians – rusty ones' (Pozner, 2017), which further distorted Goergia's assessment of its own capacity to deal with Russia and contributed to an inadequate perception of external threats.

The gravest miscalculation was that the Georgian government behaved as if it had a protective option when, in fact, it had none. The unwavering confidence that the US would step in and defend Georgia was consolidated one month before the war, when the US Secretary of State, Condoleezza Rice, went to Georgia and assured Saakashvili of the support of the US in resolving the country's tensions with Abkhazia and South Ossetia by stating that 'we will do everything that we can to help resolve these conflicts' (RT, 2008). Together with the US's active involvement in the South Caucasus, Georgia's support of

Bush's worldview and foreign policy, alliance-like military cooperation between the two countries, and the personalized nature of US-Georgia friendly relations, these reassuring statements from the top US officials made a strong and emboldening impression of the availability of a protective option for Georgia.

It must be admitted that the US made it explicit that it did not want to become involved militarily (Mouritzen & Wivel, 2012, p. 101). Washington repeatedly advised Georgia to avoid a military confrontation with Russia: 'Do not get involved in combat with Russia under any circumstances!' (Blank, 2009a, p. 118; Asmus, 2010, p. 3). In May 2008, Rice asked Burjanadze to pass a message to Saakashvili that in no way should he start, or be provoked to start, a military operation against Russia because the US would not go to war with Russia for Georgia (Pozner, 2017). However, in the broader context of US-Georgia strategic cooperation, these otherwise straightforward messages failed to remedy Georgia's grave misperception that US protection is available and Washington would intervene to save its loyal friend, at least through economic sanctions or diplomatic deterrence, if not direct military intervention. This gravely imprudent assessment of the situation resulted in Georgia's decision to attack Tskhinvali on 7 August 2008, which triggered Russia's disproportional military response.

While other factors might have also contributed to Saakashvili's decision, evidence suggests that the Georgian leader misjudged the availability of the protective option. As documented by Blank (2009b, p. 436), Saakashvili's 'ability to go around the regular channels of official communication with Washington facilitated a situation in which innocent and inadvertent statements by US officials encouraged Georgian officials who heard what they wanted to hear and allowed them to disregard other voices as not being authoritative'. Cooley and Mitchel (2009, pp. 35–36) also suggest that the 'warmth' and the increasingly personalized relationship between the two administrations in the months preceding the war should not be underestimated. While the official warnings from the US may have been clear, it was equally clear to the Georgian leadership that there would be no consequences for ignoring them (Cooley & Mitchel, 2009, p. 36). Various US officials, lobbyists, and supporters who could regularly be seen in Tbilisi sent very different messages to the Georgian government, creating a background of encouragement that Georgian leaders heard over official discouragement (Cooley & Mitchel, 2009, p. 35). Asmus (2010, pp. 141–144) documents the worries of the Swedish foreign minister Carl Bildt following his dinner with Saakashvili the evening after the NATO Bucharest summit that, despite all the warnings, the Georgian leader might have been misreading the encouraging signals from Washington. Similarly, Mouritzen and Wivel (2012, p. 74), having interviewed

Georgian Minister for Reintegration Temuri Yakobashvili and former Foreign Minister Eka Tkeshelashvili, concluded that Saakashvili and the rest of the Georgian leadership 'had apparently believed that the United States could deter Russia from the kind of large-scale invasion that took place' in August 2008. Burjanadze's statement that in 2008 Saakashvili was surrounded by people, such as Member of the Parliament Giga Bokeria, who believed that while Bush was in office, Tbilisi could proceed and resolve the Abkhazia and South Ossetia issues (Pozner, 2017) confirm these assessments. Saakashvili even suggested that Bush would decide to bomb the Russian army to defend Georgia (Pozner, 2017).

When Russia invaded Georgia on 8 August 2008, the expected support never materialized. Not only did the US and its NATO allies not engage directly, but they also refused to impose economic sanctions or intense diplomatic pressure on Russia (Asmus, 2010, p. 187). The US government stressed that the Georgia–Russia conflict would not be allowed to interfere with US–Russia cooperation on many issues of shared interests (Nichol, 2008, p. 29). Antonenko (2008, pp. 25–26) notes that 'only after Russian troops crossed into Georgia proper and started to bomb towns was the West ready to issue strong statements pressuring Russia to withdraw'. The US response, however, never went beyond the rhetorical. Once 'it was clear that Georgia had lost both Abkhazia and South Ossetia for good and the West could and would do nothing about it', the US decided to leave it to French President Nicolas Sarkozy to negotiate a cease-fire agreement between Russia and Georgia (Antonenko, 2008, p. 26). According to Mouritzen and Wivel (2012, p. 109), 'all that was left for the United States was to pick up the pieces and focus on damage control'. Soon after the war, the American Government offered to 'reset' relations with Russia and began negotiating the new Strategic Offensive Reduction Treaty in Moscow (Korolev, 2018, p. 902; Smith, 2020).

From the perspective of the Georgian government, the US let Georgia down, and Saakashvili did not try to hide his disappointment and confusion about that:

> The United States argued that Russia was bluffing, and that if it crosses the line, it would be a big mistake. But on this particular matter, it is the West that made a mistake by underestimating Russia ... I think that America must organize a resistance front among the Western countries. They have multiple levers to stop the Russian aggression. The prestige and reputation of America in the region are at stake. The reputation that the United States won after the Cold War is gradually withering away. This is tragic (Regnum, 2008).

Regardless of whether Saakashvili's criticism of the US for misguiding Tbilisi and then failing to provide the much-needed support is defensible or not, the Georgian government displayed geopolitical imprudence concerning both the dropping level of structural uncertainty and the availability of a protective option, which resulted in the dramatic foreign policy failure and the end of hedging.

3.2 Ukraine: Misreading the Structural Certainty

The 2014 Ukraine crisis is an example of hedging going awry due to geopolitical imprudence in the form of Yanukovych's idealized conception of his capacity to extract maximum benefits from both Russia and the EU. Yanukovych underestimated the dangers of adopting a primarily gains-maximizing approach to hedging under the conditions of an increasingly binary structural environment that Ukraine faced due to intensifying great power rivalry between Russia and the West and the collision between their irreconcilable geopolitical projects – the EU's Eastern Partnership and Russia's EAEU.

After becoming the president of Ukraine in February 2010, Yanukovych hedged his bets between Russia and the West by cosying up to Moscow while striving to sign an Association Agreement (AA) with the EU. Yanukovych stated: 'I intend to establish stable, strong partnerships with the European Union, Russia and the USA ... ' and 'Ukraine continues to work towards integration to the European Union ... Russia is not preventing us from implementing the reforms we are undertaking in terms of this goal ... ' (Armandon, 2011, pp. 1–2). Given Ukraine's relatively equidistant standing between Russia and the EU in terms of trade and energy relations in those years, this attempt to avoid choosing between the two poles of power was understandable from the standpoint of mitigating potential risks of deterioration of Kyiv's relations with either of the two sides. However, in the context of increasingly incompatible geopolitical agendas of Russia and the West, Kyiv prioritized gains maximization over risk mitigation, playing both Russia and the EU against each other. Such behaviour became infeasible as Ukraine's geopolitical environment was being increasingly penetrated by Russia's and EU's geopolitical interests, and Kyiv's persistent pursuit of it resulted in dramatic hedging failure.

The increasingly adversarial regional bipolar structure, formed by Russia's claim of its sphere of influence and the West's upfront rejection of it (i.e., Russia's and the West's strong intentions to balance against each other), presented Ukraine with an uncompromising 'either-or' option. After invading Georgia in 2008, Russian President Dmitri Medvedev stated that Moscow had demarcated 'a traditional sphere of Russian interests' in which it is entitled to pre-eminence (President of Russia, 2008), to which the then US Vice President Joe Biden rebutted that 'We will not recognize any nation having a sphere of influence' (The White House, 2009). The Kremlin tried to thwart the EU's expansion and expand its own sphere of influence through the EAEU, while EU members regarded the Eastern Partnership initiative, specifically the AA offered to Ukraine, as an instrument to wrest their neighbours from Moscow's grip (Charap & Colton, 2018, p. 100). When Lavrov asked, 'What is the Eastern Partnership? Is it a sphere of influence?' (Pop, 2009), some European experts wrote, 'The answer, of course, is yes ... In the post-Soviet space, neutrality is not an option for Europe .... We must face up the fact that we are engaged in a systemic competition' (Stelzenmüller, 2010). Neither Russia nor the West was public about it, but, as Smith (2020, p. 593) documented, there was certainly enough murmur to suggest that a potential win-win scenario whereby Ukraine could participate in both regional projects was infeasible. Russia and the EU were more interested in prevailing in the intensifying geopolitical rivalry than in mitigating it (Charap & Colton, 2018, p. 117). The RSC in which Ukraine found itself became increasingly certain and geopolitically charged.

The positions of Russia and the West clashed in 2011 in response to Yanukovych's attempts to hedge his bets by meeting both Moscow and the EU halfway. The head of the Customs Union Commission (the precursor of the EAEU), Sergei Glaziev, said, 'We cannot make any progress outside of the Customs Union ... The only option for Ukraine is full participation in the Customs Union. All other formulas have no basis to them, and we have informed Kyiv about that' (Kommersant.ru, 2010). In response, in December 2012, EU officials stated that it is 'impossible for Ukraine to align with both the EU and the Customs Union at the same time. Ukraine should choose which path to take ... Even partial accession to the Customs Union ... would be problematic' (Focus, 2012). The US Secretary of State Hillary Clinton chimed in by claiming: 'It [the EAEU] is not going to be called that [Soviet Union]. It's going to be called customs union, it will be called the Eurasian Union and all of that, but let's make no mistake about it. We know what the goal is, and we are trying to figure out effective ways to slow down or prevent it' (Klapper, 2012).

Moscow issued Kyiv an ultimatum when the Director of the Economic Cooperation Department of the Russian Foreign Ministry, Alexander Gorban, stated, using a somewhat metaphorical language, that 'Ukraine wants to simultaneously maintain two vectors: both to join the EU ... and to participate in the Customs Union, but only in those areas where it can gain. But things don't work that way. You cannot be just a little bit pregnant' (Newsru.com, 2012). In turn, the European Commission President Jose Manuel Barroso reminded that Ukraine could not simultaneously have a free trade area with the EU and be a member of the Customs Union with Russia: 'Our position was clearly defined ... This is not possible.' (UKRINFORM, 2013). Thus, the EU has explicitly ruled out any possibility of a trilateral arrangement involving Russia.

Russia, in turn, stated that signing the AA with the EU would be 'suicidal' for Ukraine and warned that it would tighten the customs procedures should that happen (RT, 2013). To make Ukraine abandon an EU trade accord, Russia offered Ukraine $15 billion in credits, lower gas prices, abolishing customs duties and other barriers to bilateral trade. However, should Ukraine sign the AA with the EU, it would, according to Putin's advisors, 'lose its independence' and would 'stop being a full partner' of Russia (Gotev, 2013). As Putin said in September 2013: 'We say it is your choice . . . but keep in mind that we will be forced to defend our market and implement protective measures' (President of Russia, 2013).

By that point, the geopolitical feedback offered by the RSC was clear: both competing poles of power put an 'in or out' binary choice in front of Ukraine. As noted by Smith (2020, p. 595), the bipolar geopolitical pressure reached a point where the potential to cultivate a scenario whereby Ukraine could benefit from both Russia's and the EU's regional projects was minimal and hard to achieve even for the most gifted diplomatic operators. However, Yanukovych, displaying an idealized conception of his agency in European geopolitics, was trying to precisely achieve that, hedging to reap benefits from Russia and the EU, thus becoming deeply involved in competing great powers' interests. By doing so, he failed to heed the signals from the system, misjudging both the level of structural uncertainty and the degree of protection the EU was willing to offer.

Yanukovych's political behaviour was described as a 'bulldozer' (Kutsenko, 2018), crude horse-trading (Charap & Colton, 2018, pp. 121–122), and brazen hedging (Smith, 2020) aimed at stoking EU–Russia geopolitical competition to maximize Ukraine's clout and Ukrainian elites' capacity to collect lucrative rents and pocket as many favours as possible from both Russia and the EU. Yanukovych tried to advance alignment with both powers. Such hedging seemed to work at the beginning of Yanukovych's tenure when Brussels rewarded Ukraine for creating distance from Russia through political cooperation, softer democratic conditionality, financial aid, and access to European markets, and Russia acted similarly but using its geopolitical toolkit, including manipulation of gas prices, to reward Ukraine's turn away from the EU (Tolstrup, 2014, p. 207). However, Yanukovych's gains-maximizing hedging continued when the regional environment became congested into a tighter bipolarity, indicating a lack of geopolitical prudence. In November 2012, after both Russia and the EU unequivocally ruled out any possibility of trilateral arrangements, the Ukrainian ambassador to Moscow said that 'today we don't say either yes or no to the Customs Union membership . . . but the answer will more likely be yes than no' if Ukraine's trade with the Union grows and the EU's economic problems deepen (*Zerkalo nedeli*, 2012). Yanukovych wanted to buttress his bargaining position with Brussels by demonstrating he had other options (Charap & Colton, 2018, pp. 116–117).

In May 2013, in the last stages of the AA negotiations with the EU, Ukraine signed a memorandum on cooperation with the Eurasian Economic Commission (the executive body of the EAEU), which granted Kyiv observer status. Russia interpreted it as Ukraine's firm intention to join the EAEU. According to Glaziev: 'since observer status is granted only to the states who want to join our integration project ... since we granted Ukraine this status ... that means that Ukraine intends to join our Union' (Sidorenko & Kolesnikov, 2013). Ukraine never refuted this interpretation. However, the same day the memorandum with the EAEU was signed, Yanukovych, ignoring Putin's warnings, called Barroso to reassure him that signing the memorandum did not contradict the AA and agreed to sign the agreement at the forthcoming November 2013 Vilnius summit (Charap & Colton, 2018, p. 117). Russia responded with heavy-handed measures. It imposed temporary trade sanctions on Ukraine, significantly damaging Ukrainian exports, and threatened gas price hikes to send a strong message that if Kyiv were to proceed with the AA, its bilateral ties with Russia would be significantly disrupted, which, according to some estimates, could reduce Ukraine's export to Russia by 17 per cent yearly, annually cutting Ukraine's GDP by 1.7 per cent (Charap & Colton, 2018, p. 119).

This pressure did not stop Yanukovych's attempts to squeeze benefits from both Russia and the EU. He continued pushing forward with the AA; the document's final draft was formally approved on 18 September 2013. The EU was ready to sign it despite the deterioration of democracy in Ukraine. However, while sending positive signals to the EU and pondering Brussels's willingness to provide financial compensation to offset the costs of Moscow's expected retaliation, estimated by Yanukovych at $160 billion, which the EU eventually declined, the Ukrainian leader met secretly with Putin three times in October–November to discuss the details of a financial-support package from Russia to compensate for the potential losses of not signing the AA (Koshkina, 2015, p. 25). According to Smith (2020, p. 588), such a brazen back and forth between Brussels and Moscow under the conditions of intensifying great power competition was an enactment of an idealized conception of Ukraine's actorness that ignored the stark geopolitical realities.

Instead of diversifying strategic options, Yanukovych's hedging exacerbated Russia-EU policy competition over Ukraine. Russia felt desperate about losing its sphere of influence, while the EU almost gave up on democratic conditionality, including demanding the release from prison of Yanukovych's primary political rival, Yulia Tymoshenko, to snatch Ukraine away from Moscow. Under extreme pressure from Russia, Kyiv ordered suspending the signing of the AA just a week before the Vilnius summit. However, Yanukovych continued his strategy by calling for the establishment of a 'trilateral commission' with Russia and the EU to discuss trade relations and the renewal of active dialogue with the countries of the Customs Union on trade and economic issues (Charap & Colton, 2018, p. 121). Even after signing the agreement with Moscow and committing to closer ties with Russia, Yanukovych kept telling the EU leaders that he would eventually sign the AA (Smith, 2020, p. 594).

Abruptly reneging on the promise to sign the AA with the EU triggered public protests in Kyiv that went out of control, resulting in what became known as the Maidan Revolution, which effectively plunged the country into war with Russia and ended Ukraine's hedging between Russia and the West. Ukraine also lost control over significant parts of its territory due to Russian annexation. While the external geopolitical environment that is outside of Kyiv's control weighed heavily in this unfortunate outcome and Ukraine's strategic trade-offs were never easy, Yanukovych's inflated conception of his agency vis-à-vis the larger powers resulted in imprudent judgement about the level of structural permissiveness in the region and Ukraine's capacity to juggle the stakes of great power politics that failed his hedging. The feedback from the structure, comparative evidence from Georgia, and Russia's military presence and manipulation of separatism in the former Soviet republics should have sent a powerful message incentivizing Yanukovych to, if not give up on European integration, adopt a more cautious approach to navigating great power rivalry.

Ukraine, like Georgia, also ended up without a protective option when the worst-case scenario materialized, even though Kyiv did not count on it as Tbilisi did.[14] The EU supported Ukraine during the crisis by imposing sanctions on Russia and eventually signing the AA with Kyiv. However, that was too little too late: Crimea was annexed, separatist movements in eastern Ukraine were instigated, and functional relations with Russia were destroyed, resulting in Ukraine's growing dependence on the Western military and economic help. Russia was willing to pay an enormous price to pursue its geopolitical interests in Ukraine – a price that neither the EU nor NATO was willing to consider. Neglect of security dynamics and reluctance to explicitly address the geostrategic tensions with Russia in Ukraine have been seen as significant weaknesses of the EU's approach (Raik, 2019). Economic sanctions, in turn, failed to modify Russia's course of action. The EU did not get involved directly to defend Ukraine. Nor did it or NATO provide Ukraine with explicit security guarantees.

---

[14] Considering this observation, it is possible to argue that Yanukovych's imprudence regarding structural uncertainty plaid a greater role in causing hedging failure than his or his successors' imprudence about the availability of projective option.

When Russia invaded Ukraine on 24 February 2022, the Ukraine crisis, lingering since 2014, had turned into an all-out war between Russia and Ukraine that further exemplified the lack of reliable protective options for Ukraine, resulting in a greater loss of autonomy and sovereignty. The gravity of the situation triggered multiple rounds of Western anti-Russia sanctions of unprecedented scale. A few weeks into the war, the US and its allies also started to send various weapons systems to Ukraine to buttress its combat capabilities. However, despite the US Secretary of Defense Lloyd Austin's statements in October 2021 that 'we [US and NATO] are reassuring and reinforcing the sovereignty of countries [Georgia and Ukraine] that are on the frontlines of Russian aggression' (US Department of Defence, 2021), this strong reaction falls short of the protective option necessary for preventing or averting serious harm caused to Ukraine by Russia. Either Ukraine's NATO membership or NATO's direct military involvement to defend Ukraine remained a distant prospect at the time of writing (more than two years after the invasion). While the West did support Ukraine with weapons, the provided weapons were not always the ones Ukraine needed the most, and more than two years into the war, they failed to tip the balance in favour of Ukraine on the battlefield.

Ukraine's NATO membership also remained a vague prospect. On 25 February 2022, Zelensky asked: 'Who is willing to give Ukraine a guarantee of NATO membership?' (Aljazeera, 2022). On 6 March 2022, more than a week after the invasion, UK Prime Minister Boris Johnson stated that 'Ukraine had no serious prospect of NATO membership in the near future' (Johnson, 2022). Five days later, on 11 March 2022, High Representative of the European Union for Foreign Affairs and Security Policy Josep Borrell admitted that the West had made a mistake to have promised Ukraine NATO membership: 'I am ready to admit that we made a number of mistakes ... There are moments that we could do better, there are things that we proposed and then could not implement, such as, for example, the promise that Ukraine and Georgia will become part of NATO ... I think it's a mistake to make promises that you can't keep' (Daily Sabah, 2022). On 30 September 2022, Zelensky officially applied for an expedited NATO membership. However, NATO Secretary-General Jens Stoltenberg, during his press conference in Brussels on the same day, highlighted that 'NATO is not party to the conflict' and that 'a decision on membership, of course, must be taken by all 30 allies and we take these decisions by consensus' (Jozwiak, 2022) revealing that NATO was not ready for Ukraine's membership.

NATO member states, individually or together, were also reluctant to get involved militarily to defend Ukraine. NATO Ministers of Foreign Affairs, at the extraordinary meeting in Brussels on 4 March 2022, rejected the idea of imposing a no-fly zone over Ukraine, triggering indignation of the Ukrainian leadership and Zelensky openly questioning NATO's ability to defend anyone, even its members (TASS, 2022b). According to UK Prime Minister Johnson, the war in Ukraine 'is not a NATO conflict and will not become one' (Johnson, 2022). Zelensky stated that 'we are defending Ukraine alone. Who is ready to fight alongside us? I don't see anyone ... Everyone is afraid' (Aljazeera, 2022). To Zelensky's repeated request to 'clear the sky' over Ukraine, Stoltenberg repeated that despite all the support provided to Ukraine, 'the alliance is not a party in the conflict' and, hence, will not introduce a no-fly zone (Jozwiak, 2022). In turn, Kuleba assessed that 'NATO as alliance and an institution can do very little if anything' to help Ukraine and, in fact, 'did nothing' (Bloomberg, 2022).

The West imposed unprecedented sanctions on Russia and supported Ukraine with weapons. However, economic sanctions failed to change Russia's behaviour, and the weapons were not always the ones Ukraine needed the most. More than two years into the war, they failed to tip the balance in favour of Ukraine. According to Zelensky, 'we could not resolve [with NATO] issues of delivering certain types of weapons to Ukraine', which indicates a 'lack of courage' on NATO's part (Haneneva, 2022). While the scale of military assistance was significant, it was not sufficient, and the decisions to provide more advanced types of weapons to Ukraine were slow, and, according to Zelensky's Office, 'falling far short of our real needs' (Klimova, 2022). Ukraine has lost a significant amount of strategic autonomy and sovereignty over large parts of its territory.

4 Sustaining Hedging in Southeast Asia: The Philippines, Vietnam, and Malaysia

While the Indo-Pacific differs significantly from the post-Soviet space, structural uncertainty has declined there, too. In terms of the relative capabilities of the competing great powers (the first indicator), the changes have been dramatic, leaving little confusion about the changing power distribution. In the 1990s, the total GNP of the US was almost sixteen times that of China, but by the end of the twenty-first century's second decade, China's GNP became almost 70 per cent of that of the US (World Bank, 2019). China also became the world's second-largest military budget that, according to PPP-adjusted estimates, reached more than half that of the US (Lowy Institute, 2021). The 2018 US Congressional report warned that the US's military superiority has 'eroded to a dangerous degree' so that the US 'might struggle to win, or perhaps lose, a war against China or Russia', especially 'if it is forced to fight on two or more fronts simultaneously' (National Defense Strategy Commission, 2018, pp. v–vi).

The US INDOPACOM (Indo-Pacific Command) echoed that China's military has been 'approaching parity with the United States in a number of critical areas', so 'there is no guarantee that the United States would win a future conflict with China' (U.S. Senate Armed Services Committee, 2018, p. 11). The US Indo-Pacific Strategy saw China as 'America's most consequential geopolitical challenge' and 'the only competitor with both the intent to reshape the international order and, increasingly, the economic, diplomatic, military, and technological power to do it' (White House, 2022).

The changing balance of power and the recognition of it by both great powers laid strong foundations for the formation of an increasingly penetrated, geopolitically charged Indo-Pacific RSC (the second indicator), which occurred along the broad geographic overlap of China's Belt and Road Initiative (BRI) and the US-led Indo-Pacific strategy, where both China and the US attempt to alter the regional order in their favour in both economic and security realms (Medcalf, 2014; Allison, 2017). China's growing naval activities and territorial claims in the South China Sea (SCS) have posed challenges to the freedom of the US's maritime and air navigation, thus forming the SCS subcomplex. To address new challenges, the US Defense Department changed the US Pacific Command (USPACOM) to US INDOPACOM, announcing that 'overcoming China's many challenges to a Free and Open Indo-Pacific requires a whole-of-government approach by the United States, utilising all instruments of our national power' (USINDOPACOM, 2019). In 2021, Beijing passed a new law allowing the Chinese authorities to use force against foreign ships for law enforcement purposes, meaning that the Chinese coast guards can destroy structures built by other countries on China-claimed land features (Gerstl, 2022, p. 13). In response, the US intensified demonstrations of its military might in the region. For the Chinese leaders, the US's behaviour displays clear signs of anti-China balancing (both hard and soft) to contain China (Liu, 2023). According to Singapore's Ambassador-at-large Bilahari Kausikan, 'the South China Sea has become a "proxy" for the competition between the US and China on their ideas of regional order' (Viray, 2018).

In this context, it became difficult for Southeast Asian states to manoeuvre between doing business with China and keeping security ties with the United States, as both Washington and Beijing attached more security implications to Southeast Asian countries' economic and diplomatic activities. As Suzuki and Lee (2017, p. 129) argued regarding Malaysia, 'various scenarios can be put forward as to the new strategic environment but any one will make for difficulty in the continuation of Malaysia's hedging policy'. Similar challenges have been identified with regard to the Philippines (Korolev, 2019, pp. 438–443).

However, the SCS subcomplex, embedded in the Indo-Pacific RSC, remained less intense and more uncertain compared to the post-Soviet RSC, particularly with regard to Georgia and Ukraine. Despite becoming increasingly assertive, China's approach to its claims in the SCS and the nature of its regional objectives have been characterized by 'strategic ambiguity', which blurs the exact scope of the claims and the intensity of confrontation (Zhang, 2020; Strating, 2022). Simultaneously, while both the Quadrilateral Security Dialogue between Australia, India, Japan, and the US (QUAD) and AUKUS (Australia, UK, and US) are sometimes viewed as precursors of 'Asian NATO', neither QUAD nor AUKUS entails collective defence or close coordination of military policy in pursuit of a common security goal as NATO does. They are also based on existing US-led alliances and are not an outcome of multiple rounds of expansion into another great power's area of priority strategic interests. Smaller Southeast Asian states are not part of those or other exclusive groups and, compared to Georgia and Ukraine, enjoy greater geopolitical slack when dealing with China and the US. Also, despite a shared perception among the members that China is the primary strategic challenge in the Indo-Pacific, there is no shared understanding of where that threat is most pressing and in what form (Andrews, 2024). These circumstances mitigate the precipitation of the SCS subcomplex and the Indo-Pacific RSC more broadly.

Therefore, while the Philippines, Vietnam, and Malaysia became more hard-pressed to navigate the intensifying great power rivalry, their geopolitical positions remained less contingent, exposed, and difficult due to the lower intensity of their RSC. Simultaneously, they displayed greater geopolitical prudence regarding structural uncertainty and the availability of protective options that helped them continue hedging despite the increasing US–China tensions. This suggests that they are likely to do better than Georgia and Ukraine even if the US–China rivalry in the region intensifies further. While the effectiveness of their hedging differs, all three managed to mitigate harm to sovereignty and autonomy (Table 1).

4.1 Geopolitical Prudence about Structural Uncertainty

As a starting point, the Philippines, Malaysia, and Vietnam had no illusions about their capabilities and were acutely aware of the dangers of intensifying great power rivalry, thus demonstrating a more realistic conception of their agency vis-à-vis the great powers. According to the National Security Council of the Philippines, the country's 'armed forces remain one of the weakest in Asia, putting in doubt our ability to protect and defend our sovereignty and territorial integrity' (Office of the President of the Philippines, 2018, p. 9).

Similar official self-awareness characterizes Malaysia's high-level discourse. According to former Malaysian Prime Minister Mahathir Mohamad, the country does not possess the capacity for hard balancing against China and prefers 'some other less violent ways not to antagonize China too much, because it is beneficial for us ... We realize we are a weak nation and China is a powerful nation, and, you know, powerful nations will do what they like. Weak nations will have to submit, to a certain extent' (Beddall & Yusof, 2019). Vietnam has also displayed abundant awareness of the power imbalances in the region and eschewed seeking open confrontation with China while maintaining relations with the US (Gerstl, 2022, p. 108).

The three countries displayed awareness of the risks of becoming involuntarily involved in a conflict between China and the US or being forced to bandwagon with either side. The same cannot be said about Georgia and Ukraine, which operated as if the Russia-West rivalry was not real, even when their more contentious RSC became non-permissive.

The Philippines' former president Rodrigo Duterte (2016–2022), despite his notorious populism, adopted, as Heydarian (2017, p. 2) put it, 'the mantra of pragmatism and conflict avoidance', making prevention of outright conflict in contested areas the priority of his administration, even when China deployed significant military assets to, and de-facto controlled, Scarborough Shoal and other Manila-claimed SCS areas. Moreover, right after the Hague tribunal overruled China's claims over the waters within its Nine-Dash Line in 2016, Duterte's administration decided not to capitalize on this symbolic victory, recognizing that the award 'remains unenforceable', as the then foreign minister Teodoro Locsin explained (Romero, 2019). Instead, Duterte assessed China's intentions and capabilities and ordered his diplomats to 'create an environment where we [the Philippines] can sit down and talk directly' to China; otherwise, China 'might not just even want to talk' (Heydarian, 2017, p. 2). According to Gerstl's (2022, p. 72) analysis of Duterte's public statements and interviews, Duterte and his bureaucracy were well aware of China's power and the Philippines' limited influence. They viewed Beijing's actions in the SCS as a part of a 'greater game of geopolitics' that affected the Philippines.

After the Hague tribunal ruled against China in 2016, Beijing's offer to Manila resembled Russia's binary offer to Ukraine in 2014, when Moscow tried to make Ukraine abandon the EU trade accord. Beijing made it clear that the Philippines stands to gain a lot if it eschews the confrontational strategy of the previous Aquino administration. However, it would face stark consequences if Manila leverages the arbitration award to pressure China and continues facilitating the US's military pivot to the region. Faced with the pressure, and despite being a treaty ally of the US, Manila decided to de-escalate and minimize the risks of being embroiled in a great power conflict rather than test the credibility of China's warnings. Duterte displayed determination not to provoke China: 'I will not go to war because we will not win it. It will be a massacre. I will not waste the lives of Filipino soldiers and policemen' (Heydarian, 2017). The then Secretary of National Defense, Delfin Lorenzana, stated that while the Philippines needed 'balanced ties' with both superpowers, it must avoid getting involved in their conflicts (Gerstl, 2022, p. 81). Duterte further called China a 'good' and 'fair' neighbour and agreed to shelve the sovereignty issues with China or address them through bilateral negotiations (de Castro, 2022). 'If it costs a third world war, what might be the point of insisting on the ownership of the waters? It does not bring prosperity', Duterte said (Huang & Steger, 2016).

Duterte administration did not give up on its alliance with the US but modified and refashioned the joint bilateral military exercises with the US that were perceived as directed against China to avoid provoking Beijing. This included the suspension of joint patrols and major military exercises in the SCS in exchange for improved economic and diplomatic ties with China, including a modus vivendi in the disputed areas (Heydarian, 2017, p. 14). Thus, instead of trying to align with both great powers, as Ukraine's Yanukovych did towards Russia and the EU, Duterte made it clear that he would not side with the US to balance against China because, he believed, the US's stronger military engagement in the Indo-Pacific might cause a direct conflict with China in the SCS that would spiral out of control and crush the Philippines (de Castro, 2022; Gerstl, 2022, p. 72). He signalled that while security cooperation with Washington is important, a stronger US military presence in the region may not improve the national security of the Philippines. While this policy has not resolved the Philippines' strategic dilemmas, it has helped Manila navigate the great power rivalry and mitigate its risks.

Another Southeast Asian state – Malaysia – has been known for its championship of regionalism, which helped to insulate Southeast Asia from great power rivalry. The Malaysian government made the issue of navigating the US–China rivalry a top foreign policy priority and tried not to upset either side. Malaysia demonstrated prudence regarding its geopolitical environment, trying to minimize risks, which proved a workable hedging strategy.

Malaysia downplayed the negative impact of the SCS dispute and assuaged China's assertiveness by displaying respect towards China's role in global politics. Mahathir pursued a 'quiet strategy' and a 'low-key approach' (Suzuki & Lee, 2017, p. 115) in the SCS to avoid fuelling China–US rivalry. He favoured the status quo while criticizing the internationalization of the SCS territorial disputes (Gerstl, 2022, pp. 49–53). Mahathir also downplayed the occasional face-offs with China over territorial claims and the associated security risks while being willing to meet China halfway (Suzuki & Lee, 2018; Gerstl, 2022). Malaysia prioritized the more universal UNCLOS (United Nations Convention on the Law of the Sea) instead of the more region-specific and controversial CoC (Code of Conduct for the SCS) as an instrument of conflict resolution. This step helped avoid conflicts over regional rule-making (Suzuki & Lee, 2018). While these measures did not resolve the SCS dispute, they helped Malaysia avoid antagonizing China while maintaining good relations with the US.

Aware of the increasing irreconcilability of alignment with the US and strong partnerships with China, Malaysia avoided brandishing strategic cooperation with Washington and consistently reassured Beijing that it would not join any attempt to contain China. In contrast to Ukraine's unquestioning posture towards the European Association agreement that irritated Russia, Malaysia openly questioned Obama's Trans-Pacific Partnership (TPP) as being unfair to smaller states and 'taking a stand that is almost anti-Chinese' (Council on Foreign Relations, 2018). This helped mitigate Beijing's concerns about the rise of anti-China geoeconomic blocks in the Indo-Pacific. Mahathir criticized Washington's power projection in the SCS but quietly supported US involvement in the region without becoming a formal US ally (Pakiam, 2019, p. 206). Recognizing Beijing's sensitivity towards the US's geopolitical initiatives in the Indo-Pacific, Malaysia viewed closer cooperation with Washington as a source of potential risks, and its close military cooperation with it was deliberately kept low-key with no intention of a military alliance (Kuik, 2013). Nor did Mahathir criticize China regarding Xinjiang, mentioning China's supreme power and warning against doing 'something that will fail, and in the process, also, we will suffer' (Gerstl, 2022, p. 56). Suzuki and Lee (2018) argue that China-aware behaviour is not unique to Mahathir but also characterizes the administrations of Abdullah Badawi (2003–2009) and Najib Razak (2009–2018).

Along with displaying greater sensitivity to China's geopolitical interests and keeping cooperation with the US low profile, Malaysia's hedging also involves pursuing equidistance between China and the US and explicitly uttering concerns about *both* great powers. Such an approach helped mitigate risks, in contrast to the more brazen gains-maximization behaviour of Saakashvili's Georgia and Yanukovych's Ukraine under greater external pressure. Malaysian former foreign minister Saifuddin Abdullah emphasized in 2019 that 'both superpowers are there in the South China Sea without invitation from any of the ASEAN member states' and that both must be aware that 'as much as we are not going to stop them from being there, we are also not very pleased that both of them are too active in the region' (Bland, 2019). Eight years earlier, in

June 2011, at the 10th Shangri-La Dialogue in Singapore, the then Malaysian Prime Minister Najib Razak openly expressed his concerns about the growing possibility of great power rivalry in the region and emphasized that while both China and the US are Malaysia's partners, 'it is not about taking sides. We must replace the old bilateralism of the Cold War not with a new bilateralism, but a multilateralism that can rise to the task ahead' (Kuik, 2013, p. 159). Malaysia also responded cautiously to the AUKUS pact and the associated submarine deal, warning that it might trigger 'a nuclear arms race in the Indo-Pacific region' and 'provoke other powers to act more aggressively in the region, especially in the South China Sea' (New Straits Times, 2021). While the sustainability of Malaysia's hedging can be questioned, prudent reading of great power rivalry has helped Malaysia avoid siding with either China or the US or becoming involved in the strategic rivalry between them.

The third case – Vietnam – also displays prudence about its structural environment. Hanoi's awareness of the limits of its capacity vis-à-vis China and the dangers of becoming entrapped in the China–US rivalry is manifested in how it views China and engages with China and the US. As Hai (2017, p. 1) demonstrates, Hanoi views China's power as a 'constant feature of political life' in Vietnam and constantly tries to live with it and benefit from it. Thayer (2002, p. 271) captures this in his 'tyranny of geography' concept, according to which the Vietnamese are fully aware of their 'geographic misfortune' of bordering on China and try to find ways to coexist with their giant neighbour. Similarly, Hai and Kim (2017, p. 197) describe Vietnamese's perception of China as a 'force of nature' like floods and storms that feed into the deltas and 'to which Vietnamese, like reeds, must once bend while remaining firmly intact'. Such a force can be 'terrifying and destructive', but when harnessed, it can be 'nourishing and productive' (Hai & Kim, 2017, p. 197). China is like a 'tide' that Vietnam can ride if it is aware of the potential dangers and adjusts its behaviour accordingly (Hai, 2017). This way of approaching China differs from Ukraine's and Georgia's bolder approach to Russia, even though the latter can also be viewed as an element of the 'tyranny of geography'.

Aware of its positionality vis-à-vis China, Vietnam's leadership has tried to maintain a pragmatic and flexible dialogue with Beijing and promote cooperation to mitigate risks in bilateral relations (Gerstl, 2022, p. 96). While the elites are divided on how exactly to maintain relations with China – whether through shared socialist ideology or economic, political, and defence-security enmeshment – all agree on the necessity to do that (Thayer 2017, p. 2), which explains why Vietnam has refrained from actions that China would deem confrontational, such as actively pursuing international legal arbitration in the SCS. Even during tense episodes in the bilateral relationship when structural uncertainty seemed to disappear, such as after the 2014 Haiyuan Shiyou 981 oil rig crisis that involved Chinese vessels ramming Vietnamese ships, the Vietnamese called on China to discuss the management of the incident and, after China withdrew the oil rig, started reconciling with Beijing, pushing for more dialogue and cooperation (Hai, 2017).

Like Malaysia, Vietnam opted for low-profile cooperation with the US not to provoke China. It assured China that it had no intention to align with Washington to balance against China's rise. Thus, in 2013, Vietnam did not agree to a strategic partnership with the US even though officials from both sides considered the idea (Gerstl, 2022, p. 115). Instead, Vietnam favoured just a Joint Statement on Comprehensive Strategic Cooperation (Thayer, 2017, p. 6). Being aware of the sources of threats and reluctant to test the capacity and intentions of China, Vietnam persisted with its 'three no's' policy (no foreign troops on Vietnamese soil, no allying with one country to counter another, and no military alliances with foreign powers) and, while generally supporting US's presence in the SCS, restricted the extent to which it cooperates with the US by insisting on conducting only 'naval exchange activities', as distinct from 'naval exercises', with the US Navy (Thayer, 2017, p. 13). The US's attempt in 2023 to formally upgrade ties with Vietnam to commemorate the 10th anniversary of the Joint Statement on Comprehensive Strategic Cooperation faced resistance in Hanoi due to the intensifying China–US competition and Hanoi's reluctance to be part of it (Guarascio, 2023). Like Malaysia and the Philippines, and unlike Georgia and Ukraine, Vietnam trod the great power relations carefully and managed to sustain its hedging (Table 1).

4.2 Prudence and Approaches to Protective Options

The Philippines, Malaysia, and Vietnam are different in their alignment arrangements. However, the way the three states approach alignment with the competing great powers (China and the US) is different from how Georgia and Ukraine manoeuvred between Russia and the West. Unlike their post-Soviet counterparts, they were cautious and reluctant to take bold moves without explicit confirmation of security guarantees.

Despite being a US treaty ally, the Philippines questioned Washington's defence commitment when facing intensifying US–China rivalry, seeking confirmation of the US's willingness to fight for the Philippines if need be. This starkly contrasts Saakashvili's Georgia, which, in a much more pressing situation, assumed US military support that never materialized. Manila became hesitant about the availability of a protective option after the US failed to explicitly guarantee its military support in the event of conflict over disputed features within the Philippines' 200-nautical-mile exclusive economic zone (EEZ) and repeatedly equivocated on whether the two countries' Mutual Defense Treaty (MDT) covers the Philippines' territorial disputes in the SCS (Heydarian, 2017). Washington did not deter China in the Scarborough Reef standoff in April–June 2012 and failed to enforce the China–Philippines mutual withdrawal agreement. Despite de-escalating, China did not fully disengage and eventually took complete control of the shoal. The US conducted regular aerial surveillance and maritime patrols in the area, but that was not enough to stop China. More broadly, the US struggled to uphold the rule of law and prevent China from building massive artificial islands in the region.

While it is convenient to write Duterte's behaviour off to his persona or idiosyncrasies within the Philippines' domestic politics, the ambiguity of the US's security guarantees, concerns regarding the US's reliability as an ally and its inability to change China's behaviour in the region, and the imperative to avoid a military confrontation with Beijing, incentivized Duterte to be more prudent about the availability of protective option when dealing with US–China rivalry. Manila did not take the US's support and reliability for granted, and Duterte raised concerns about the reliability of his treaty ally. Some argued that the 'obstacles of geography' faced by the US, unlike the PRC, also contributed to Duterte's reassessment and open questioning of American security guarantees should war erupt in the SCS (Andrade, 2020). Moreover, Duterte openly questioned American security guarantees should war erupt in the SCS by stressing that the 1951 MDT did not guarantee US support in a crisis and questioning the Philippine-US Enhanced Defense Cooperation Agreement (EDCA) signed by the two allies in 2014. In the context of China enhancing its de facto control of the SCS, the then Secretary of Defense Lorenzana also asked the US to clarify the scope of application of its defence obligations under the 1951 MDT (de Castro, 2022). According to Duterte, 'America has failed us . . . the US will not fight to die for us . . . I would only ask the US ambassador, "Are you with us [in the South China Sea]?"' (Heydarian, 2017, p. 2). In this context, Duterte attempted to diversify his security options by engaging in a more multifaceted foreign policy by reaching out to China and Russia – 'I will be chartering a new course on its own and will not be dependent on the United States' (Heydarian, 2017, p. 1).

Duterte may not have done exceptionally well in forging the Philippines' relations with China and the US. Some might consider his behaviour clumsy, reckless, counterproductive, and driven primarily by political populism rather than prudence. Moreover, his foreign policy can be viewed as a contingent consequence of the shift in US strategy following the election of Donald Trump in 2016. However, the fact remains that when the external geopolitical environment became challenging, whether due to Trump's own populism or not, Duterte and his diplomats decided to reassess and re-cultivate Manila's protective options instead of taking them for granted. Without explicit confirmation from Washington that the US would defend the Philippines in a war with China, the Duterte administration decided not to test the US commitments and preferred not to continue antagonizing China. If the US's failure to stop China in the SCS was a sufficient reason for the Philippines to question the availability of a protective option, why did the EU's and US's incapacity to stop Russia's provocations fail to send a warning call to Georgia and Ukraine, prompting them to exercise caution? The two post-Soviet states, especially Georgia in 2008, acted like they had rock-solid security guarantees against Russia's invasion, which was never the case.

Duterte's foreign policy manoeuvring had worked because the US responded with reassurances and clarifications of its commitments to MDT and the implementation of the 2014 EDCA. When visiting Manila in March 2019, US Secretary of State Michael Pompeo said: 'As the South China Sea is part of the Pacific, any armed attack on Philippine forces, aircraft or public vessels in the South China Sea will trigger mutual defence obligations under Article 4 of our mutual defence treaty' (Panda, 2019). In separate talks with Duterte, Pompeo stated that 'our commitments under the treaty are clear. Our obligations are real.' (Manila Bulletin, 2019). In November 2020, the Philippines suspended the Philippine-US Visiting Forces Agreement (VFA) termination, initiated earlier by Duterte, which arguably placed the alliance on a firmer footing. The Biden Administration was quick to reaffirm security commitments to the Philippines and the MDT specifically and deployed U.S.S. Theodore Roosevelt and the U.S.S. Makin into the SCS in early April 2021 for operations in support of a 'free and open Indo-Pacific' (de Castro, 2022). In July 2021, the US Secretary of Defence, Lloyd Austin, thanked Duterte for his decision regarding the VFA and called the Philippines a 'vital treaty ally' (Dziedzic, 2021). Having reconfirmed its protective option, the Philippines continued to hedge instead of bandwagoning with China, which might have happened had it not had the protective option.

The successive Ferdinant Marcos Jr. administration took measures to strengthen the alliance with the United States in the context of deteriorating relations with China and Joe Biden's attempts to reinforce the US's Indo-Pacific alliances to counter China. Instead of focusing on domestic anti-insurgency operations, Marcos prioritized external defence and approved a wider US military presence in the Philippines by allowing rotating groups of American military forces to stay in four more Philippine military camps. This decision allowed US forces to establish staging grounds and surveillance posts in the northern Philippines across the channel from Taiwan and in western Philippine provinces facing the SCS. On 22–26 April 2024, for the first time in years, the annual US–Philippines combat-readiness exercises took place within the contested Spratly Islands and included sinking a mock enemy ship and practising a scenario of a foreign invasion of the Philippine archipelago, indicating a step forward in US–Philippines defence cooperation and increasing concerns over China's increasingly assertive actions. China strongly opposes the exercises and the growing US–Philippines military cooperation. The Philippines' authorities, in turn, stated that the alliance with the US and the joint exercises are 'very important to show China that you may have all the ships that you have, but we have a lot of firepower to sink all of them' (Associated Press, 2024). This shift has reestablished the protective option in the form of a military alliance with the US and made balancing elements in Manila's China policy more pronounced, arguably marking a transition from hedging to balancing.

Malaysia and Vietnam do not have treaty allies and, therefore, cannot easily transition from hedging to balancing. However, they have displayed prudence in their approaches to potential protective option arrangements. Careful not to incur hostilities, they tried to mitigate the risk of having to make binary choices between China and the US and extend their hedging space by reaching out to other significant actors. In contrast, Georgia and Ukraine became locked up between irreconcilable Russia and the West without reaching out to other powers and regional multilateral platforms.

Malaysia maintained equidistance between China and the US instead of trying to deepen engagement with both great powers to reap maximum benefits; the latter was Yanukovych's course of action that led Kyiv into a buzz-saw of Russia-West rivalry. Despite the US being the only power that can credibly balance China in Southeast Asia, the Malaysian government recognized that a closer alignment with the US would reduce the chances of Malaysia benefitting from China's economic growth and make the overall geopolitical environment more uncompromising. Malaysia acted to send a subtle warning to China that Malaysia welcomes the US's presence in the region but also that it would not overstep what is 'acceptable'. Malaysian Defence Minister Hishammuddin bin Hussein explicitly denied that Malaysia would allow US spy planes to take off from the Malaysian base in Sabah. Doing so reassured China that strengthening Malaysia's relations with the US was not directed against China (Suzuki & Lee, 2018, p. 122). Malaysia also clarified that cooperation with Japan is welcomed only in the economic sphere and ruled out the possibility of any security alliance with Tokyo (Suzuki & Lee, 2018, p. 122). Thus, Malaysia managed to keep cultivating a relationship with the US as a possible protective option against Beijing while keeping amicable relations with the latter, making room for hedging.

Vietnam is an example of consistent attempts to diversify strategic partnerships to circumvent the binary – US or China – geopolitical configuration and thus insulate itself from US–China rivalry. Hanoi tried to strengthen its ties with the US. However, unsure about the degree of support the US may provide in Vietnam's open confrontation with China, it did it within a broader context of diversifying its strategic partnerships. Shortly after US Secretary of Defense Lloyd Austin and US Vice President Kamala Harris visited Hanoi in August 2021, Vietnamese Prime Minister Pham Minh Chinh had a meeting with Chinese Ambassador Xiong Bo in which he reassured Beijing that 'Vietnam does not align itself with one country against any other' (Kuik, 2021, p. 8). This concurs with Emmerson's (2020a, p. 30) argument that 'it makes sense for Vietnam and other member states to look for extra-regional partners while improving their national capacities for physical deterrence ... '. As a senior member of the Politburo, Dinh The Huynh, stated during his visit to Washington in 2016, Vietnam would like to work with the US and relevant countries 'to boost ASEAN's central role and build ASEAN-led mechanisms to form regional architecture in the 21st century', emphasizing Vietnam's hope for 'the active role of countries inside and outside the region' in keeping peace and stability in the SCS (VietnamNet, 2016).

Driven by these considerations, Vietnam has established sixteen strategic partnerships and ten comprehensive partnerships with various countries, including Australia and the US (Thayer, 2017, p. 4). Quite telling was Hanoi's foreign policy gambit of reaching out to Russia on 30 November 2021, when Vietnamese President Nguyen Xuan Phuc visited Moscow to meet with Putin and consolidate the bilateral comprehensive strategic partnership. In a joint statement following the meeting, both parties pledged to deepen cooperation in defence and security by broadening bilateral contacts and strengthening cooperation in military personnel training (TASS, 2021). Reaching out to another great power (Russia) when intensifying US–China rivalry increasingly corners Hanoi into a binary choice is an attempt to foster a multipolar environment and create an extra hedge in relations with China and the US.

This hedging logic is also reflected in Putin's visit to Hanoi on 20 June 2024. Despite risking angering the US, Vietnamese President To Lam welcomed Putin two years after Russia's invasion of Ukraine and announced that Putin had contributed to 'peace, stability and development' in the Asia-Pacific region and the world and that the two countries wanted 'to push up' defence and security cooperation (Ratcliffe, 2024). The two leaders were also reported to have signed more than a dozen bilateral cooperation agreements and had discussions about creating 'a reliable security architecture in the Asia-Pacific', expressing 'identical or very close' positions on key international issues (Strangio, 2024).

According to some reports, security issues and arms trade were the paramount reasons for Putin's visit, even with Russian and Vietnamese media focusing mainly on economic cooperation (Hutt, 2024).

While Russia is an unlikely protective option in the sense that it can hardly 'protect' Vietnam militarily if its hedging involving China and the US fails, the breadth and depth of Moscow's strategic cooperation with both Beijing and Hanoi put Russia in a unique geopolitical position, making it more valuable for Vietnam than just a regular arms and energy trade partner. As emphasized by Victor Sumsky, director of the ASEAN Centre at the Moscow Institute of International Affairs, in the context of the SCS dispute, 'special relations with both Beijing and Hanoi are a resource that should not be underestimated', and the 'Moscow needs to think more about how to neutralize . . . unhappy trends' in the region (Sumsky, 2012). Some Russian experts even argued that Russia should show consistency in its partnership relations with Vietnam and encourage the formation of some sort of China–Vietnam alignment (Mosyakov, 2013). In the context of intensifying US–China rivalry, Beijing is willing to accept Russia–Vietnam military cooperation, even though reluctantly, because it helps slow down the strengthening of Vietnam–US alignment. A termination or decline of large-scale arms sales by Russia to Vietnam would lead to the latter's stronger tilt towards the US. This explains why, despite resisting the internationalization of the SCS dispute and pressuring American, Indian, and Malaysian energy companies not to cooperate with Vietnam in the SCS, China remains largely silent about Russia's involvement in Vietnam's offshore energy projects (Torode, 2011).

Vietnam, as a hedger, understands that. While competing with China over the SCS, Hanoi also tries to cooperate with China. A close strategic partnership with Russia creates new channels for engagement with Beijing and helps mitigate potential risks of escalation. Vietnam's Russia policy is not simply an attempt to fence off the Chinese threat. Unlike the US, Japan, or other partners, Russia remains close to China, so strategic cooperation with Moscow not only provides Hanoi with the required access to energy technologies and advanced military hardware but also creates an extra gateway for engaging with China. In contrast, closer cooperation with the US would result in taking a side in the US–China rivalry, which would mean a confrontation with China.

The discussion of the Philippines', Malaysia's, and Vietnam's approaches to protective options requires mentioning the role of ASEAN, which provides the three countries not only with a platform for regular meetings and negotiations but also a tool for directly engaging Beijing, mediating and managing the territorial disputes with China, and indirectly balancing against it – which makes ASEAN a quasi-protective option. Thus, the Philippines, while promoting direct bilateral

Table 1 Summary of the case studies

Cases → Hedging ↓	Georgia	Ukraine	Philippines	Vietnam	Malaysia
Hedging outcome	**Failure**: loss of both territory and autonomy	**Failure**: loss of both territory and autonomy	**Partial success**: intensifying territorial dispute with China and declining autonomy due to consolidating Philippines–US alliance	**Success**: intensifying territorial dispute with China but preservation of autonomy	**Success**: contained territorial dispute with China and preservation of autonomy
Structural uncertainty	**Absent**: clear power distribution and consolidated, geopolitically charged RSC	**Absent**: clear power distribution and consolidated, geopolitically charged RSC	**Disappearing**: clear power distribution and precipitating RSC	**Disappearing**: clear power distribution and precipitating RSC	**Disappearing**: clear power distribution and precipitating RSC
Protective option	**Unavailable**: key security partner (the US) failed to protect in conflict.	**Unavailable**: key partners (US, EU) failed to protect in conflict; later support fell short of expectations and needs	**Available**: consolidating peacetime military alliance with the US untested in the absence of war with China.	**Unknown**: multiple security partnerships with no binding security commitments; consolidating military cooperation with Russia and the US	**Unknown**: security partnerships with no binding alliances or visible security commitments or inclinations.

Table 1 (cont.)

Cases → Hedging ↓	Georgia	Ukraine	Philippines	Vietnam	Malaysia
Prudence	**Imprudent**: inaccurate assessment of geopolitical environment and dramatic misjudgement of protective option	**Imprudent**: inaccurate assessment of protective option and dramatic misjudgement of geopolitical environment	**Prudent**: prudent assessment of geopolitical environment and protective option	**Prudent**: prudent assessment of geopolitical environment and protective option	**Prudent**: prudent assessment of geopolitical environment and protective option
Main actors involved	Russia, US/NATO	Russia, EU, US/NATO	China, US	China, US, Russia, ASEAN	China, US, ASEAN

engagement with China on the SCS, still uses ASEAN mechanisms as the main multilateral channel for talks and negotiations on the dispute and, for that, articulates its position in line with the wording and phrasing of ASEAN (Gerstl, 2022, pp. 77, 85). Malaysia, too, utilizes its important role within ASEAN to strengthen its bargaining position and promote its interests in the SCS vis-à-vis China. The then Malaysian Deputy Prime Minister Anwar Ibrahim, when elaborating on how Southeast Asian Nations can best defend their territory against China, stated that 'the best option is to work with other small countries in ASEAN to defend our security position' (Radio Free Asia, 2019). This is why Malaysia strongly supports the ASEAN–China negotiations on the CoC, supports ASEAN-led patrols of the SCS, and uses ASEAN to conduct talks with leading Japanese and American politicians (Gerstl, 2022, p. 56). Similarly, Vietnam regularly cites ASEAN's position when stressing its national interests and uses ASEAN forums and channels to multilateralize the SCS dispute (Do, 2017, pp. 95–123).

5 Conclusion

The main goal of this study was to identify the causes of hedging failure in the behaviour of smaller powers under the conditions of intensifying great power rivalry. The theoretical model offered in the study has highlighted the importance of three key causal variables – structural uncertainty, availability of protective options, and decision-maker's geopolitical prudence – and the interaction between them in determining hedging outcomes. Structural uncertainty is directly hinged on the degree of systemic pressure generated by great power rivalry. It affects the overall space and feasibility of hedging. When the international system is not dominated by great power competition, hedging is easier, and the need for protective options and policymaking prudence is less urgent. When great power competition intensifies, and regional environments into which it trickles down become increasingly contentious, the need for both protective options and geopolitical prudence increases.

While the level of structural uncertainty is beyond smaller states' control and the availability of protective options is not entirely in their control, it is geopolitical prudence, understood as the way smaller powers assess both the level of structural uncertainty and the availability of protective options, that mitigates the constraining impact of structural factors. This analysis has demonstrated how higher prudence in the form of a risk-mitigating approach to hedging helped Southeast Asian states, such as the Philippines, Malaysia, and Vietnam, sustain their hedging behaviour. In contrast, lower levels of prudence, that is, a gains-maximizing approach to hedging in Ukraine and Georgia, led to hedging failure when great power rivalry intensified, and the RSC in which these countries resided became heavily penetrated by larger powers' interests. To hedge successfully, smaller powers must be acutely aware of the limits of their actorness and the support external powers are willing to provide. Inaccurately assessing the latter while overestimating the former leads to the most detrimental outcomes.

However, even with highly prudent leaders, hedging may not be a sustainable foreign policy option. As systemic pressure increases and structural uncertainty disappears, hedging will become increasingly difficult, and there are reasons to expect signs of transition from hedging to behaviour patterns resembling balancing or bandwagoning. Nevertheless, the room for hedging is shrinking more for some smaller states than others. As defined in this article, geopolitical prudence helps generate foreign policy wiggle room, avoid involuntary alignments, and extend hedging opportunities. The five case studies demonstrated that finding the right balance between minimizing risks and maximizing benefits when the international environment becomes increasingly contentious is not a trivial task. The key difference between the cases of the Philippines, Malaysia, and Vietnam, on the one hand, and Georgia and Ukraine, on the other, is that even though navigating more permissive conditions, the three Southeast Asian states place a stronger emphasis on mitigating risks and maintaining relatively equal distance from both China and the US instead of maximizing gains and pursuing equally deep engagement with the two great powers – something that Ukraine under Yanukovych tried to achieve under more contentious RSC. Future research will need to pay more attention to further conceptual delineation of these two different logics of hedging – minimizing risks by eschewing sensitive areas of cooperation and maximizing benefits by matching a deeper engagement with one great power with deeper engagement with the other – and how they operate under different levels of structural uncertainty. The suggested framework can also be tested and refined through application to other cases, such as, for instance, Hungary in Eastern Europe and Singapore in Southeast Asia as examples of states that consistently hedged since 2010.

References

Aljazeera (2022, February 25). We're defending Ukraine alone, says President Zelenskyy. www.aljazeera.com/news/2022/2/25/we-are-defending-our-state-alone-says-ukraines-president.

Allison, G. (2017). *Destined for War: Can America and China Escape Thucydides' Trap?* New York: Houghton Mifflin Harcourt.

Andrade, J. I. (2020, August 11). PH Needs to Balance Ties with China, US – Lorenzana. *Inquirer.Net*, https://newsinfo.inquirer.net/1319712/ph-needs-to-balance-ties-with-china-us-lorenzana.

Andrews, D. M. (2024, 22 March). Faux-Alliances: AUKUS and the Quad are No Asian NATO, Australian Institute of International Affairs, www.internationalaffairs.org.au/australianoutlook/faux-alliances-aukus-and-the-quad-are-no-asian-nato/.

Antonenko, O. (2008). A war with no winners. *Survival*, *50*(5), 23–36.

Armandon, E. (2011, September 26). Ukraine-European Union Relations since the election of Viktor Yanukovych. *European Issues*, *12*, 1–6.

Asmus, R. (2010). *A Little War That Shook the World: Georgia, Russia, and the Future of the West*. New York: Palgrave MacMillan.

Associated Press (2024, May 9). 'US and Philippine forces sink a ship during largescale drills in the disputed South China Sea', www.9news.com.au/world/us-philippine-forces-sink-ship-during-south-china-sea-drills-australian-air-force-surveillance/0dd9ff8e-42fc-4674-b6c7-6fbf6792137f?ref.

Beddall, K., & Yusof, N. (2019, September 27). In Interview, Malaysian PM Speaks on China, Regional Balance of Power, Race Politics. *BenarNews*, www.benarnews.org/english/news/malaysian/question-answer-09272019150003.html.

Beeson, M., & Higgott, R. (2014). The changing architecture of politics in the Asia-Pacific: Australia's middle power moment? *International Relations of the Asia-Pacific*, *14*(2), 215–237.

Berg, E., & Kuusk, E. (2010). What makes sovereignty a relative concept? Empirical approaches to international society. *Political Geography*, *29*(1), 40–49.

Bland, B (2019, December 4). In Conversation: Malaysia's Foreign Minister on Great Power Rivalry. Conversation with Ben Bland. *The Interpreter*, www.lowyinstitute.org/the-interpreter/conversation-malaysias-foreign-minister-great-power-rivalry.

Blank, S. (2009a). From neglect to duress: The west and the Georgian crisis before the 2008 war. In Svante E. Cornell & S. Frederick Starr (eds.), *The Guns of August 2008: Russia's War in Georgia*, (pp. 104–121). Armonk, NY: Sharpe.

Blank, S. (2009b). America and the Russo-Georgian war. *Small Wars & Insurgencies*, *20*(2), 425–451.

Bloomberg (2022, May 16). Ask Russia About Ceasefire Terms, Not Ukraine: FM Kuleba. www.bloomberg.com/news/videos/2022-05-16/ask-russia-about-ceasefire-terms-not-ukraine-fm-kuleba-video.

Buzan, B., & Wæver, O. (2003). *Regions and Powers: The Structure of International Security*. Cambridge: Cambridge University Press.

Chan, L. H. (2019). *Australia's Strategic Hedging in the Indo-Pacific: A 'Third Way' beyond either China or the US*. Sydney: Australia-China Relations Institute.

Chang, J. Y. (2022). Not between the devil and the deep blue sea: Singapore's hedging. *International Studies Quarterly*, *66*(3), sqac034.

Charap, S., & Colton, T. J. (2018). *Everyone Loses: The Ukraine Crisis and the Ruinous Contest for Post-Soviet Eurasia*. London: Routledge.

Chung, J. H. (2009/2010). East Asia responds to the rise of China: patterns and variations. *Pacific Affairs*, *82*(4), 657–675.

Ciorciari, J. D. (2009). The balance of great-power influence in contemporary Southeast Asia. *International Relations of the Asia-Pacific*, *9*(1), 157–196.

Ciorciari, J. D. (2019). The variable effectiveness of hedging strategies. *International Relations of the Asia-Pacific*, *19*(3), 523–555.

Ciorciari, J. D., & Haacke, J. (2019). Hedging in international relations: An introduction. *International Relations of the Asia-Pacific*, *19*(3), 367–374.

Cooley, A., & Mitchell, L. A. (2009). No way to treat our friends: Recasting recent US–Georgian relations. *The Washington Quarterly*, *32*(1), 27–41.

Council on Foreign Relations (2018). A Conversation with Mahathir Mohamad. 26 September. www.cfr.org/event/conversation-mahathir-mohamad.

Daily Sabah. (2022, March 11). West made mistake in promising Ukraine NATO membership: Borrell. www.dailysabah.com/world/europe/west-made-mistake-in-promising-ukraine-nato-membership-borrell.

De Castro, R. C. (2022). Caught between appeasement and limited hard balancing: The Philippines' changing relations with the eagle and the dragon. *Journal of Current Southeast Asian Affairs*, *41*(2), 258–278.

Do, T. H. (2017). *Vietnam and the South China Sea: Politics, Security and Legality*. London: Routledge.

Dueck, C. (2005). Realism, culture, and grand strategy: Explaining America's peculiar path to world power. *Security Studies*, *14*(2), 195–231.

Dziedzic, S. (2021, July 30). President Rodrigo Duterte Abandons Plans to End Crucial Defence Deal between Philippines and the United States. ABC Premium News. https://www.abc.net.au/news/2021-07-30/philippines-defence-deal-biden-visiting-forces-agreement/100338062.

Eckstein, H. (1991). Case study and theory in political science. In H. Eckstein (ed.), *Regarding Politics: Essays on Political Theory, Stability, and Change*. Berkley: University of California Press.

Emmerson, D. K. (2020a). The Deer and the Dragon. Asymmetry versus Autonomy. In D. K. Emmerson (ed.), *The Deer and the Dragon: Southeast Asia and China in the 21st Century*, (pp. 1–40). Stanford: The Walter H. Shorenstein Asia-Pacific Research Center.

Fiammenghi, D., Rosato, S., Parent, J. M. et al. (2018). Correspondence: Neoclassical realism and its critics. *International Security*, *43*(2), 193–203.

Focus. (2012, December 25). ES: Lebot ychastie Ukrainu v Tavzhennom Coyuze nesvmestimo s dal'neishei evrointegraciei [European Union: any participation of Ukraine in the Custom Union is incompatible with its further integration with Europe]. https://focus.ua/politics/255133.

Foot, R. (2006). Chinese strategies in a US-hegemonic global order: Accommodating and hedging. *International Affairs*, *82*(1), 77–94.

Fordham, B. O. (2012). The limits of neoclassical realism: Additive and interactive approaches to explaining foreign policy preferences. In N. M. Ripsman, J. W. Taliaferro, & S. E. Lobell (eds.), *Neoclassical Realism* (pp. 251–79). Cambridge: Cambridge University Press.

Fortier, M., & Massie, J. (2023). Strategic hedgers? Australia and Canada's defence adaptation to the global power transition. *International Journal*, *78*(3), 463–478.

Garlick, J., & Havlová, R. (2020). China's 'Belt and Road' economic diplomacy in the persian gulf: Strategic hedging amidst Saudi–Iranian regional rivalry. *Journal of Current Chinese Affairs*, *49*(1), 82–105. 1868102619898706.

George, A. (1979). Case studies and theory development: The method of structured, focused comparison. In P. G. Lauren (ed.), Diplomacy: *New Approaches in History, Theory, and Policy*. New York: Free Press, 43–68.

Gerstl, A. (2022). *Hedging Strategies in Southeast Asia*. London: Routledge.

Goh, E. (2005). Meeting the China challenge: the U.S. in Southeast Asian regional security strategies. *Policy Studies*, No. 16. Washington, D.C.: East-West Center. https://scholarspace.manoa.hawaii.edu/server/api/core/bitstreams/8b1d6403-f890-4e4d-90f0-9fa9e708303a/content.

Goh, E. (2006). Understanding 'hedging' in Asia-Pacific security. PacNet 43, 31 August 2006.

Goldman, E. O. (2011). *Power in Uncertain Times: Strategy in the Fog of Peace*. Stanford, CA: Stanford University Press.

Gotev, G. (2013, September 4). EU loses Armenia to Russia's Customs Union. *Euractiv*. www.euractiv.com/section/europe-s-east/news/eu-loses-armenia-to-russia-s-customs-union/.

Götz, E. (2019). Enemy at the gates: A neoclassical realist explanation of Russia's Baltic policy. *Foreign Policy Analysis*, *15*(1), 99–117.

Götz, E. (2021). Neoclassical realist theories, intervening variables, and paradigmatic boundaries. *Foreign Policy Analysis*, *17*(2), oraa026.

Guarascio, F. (2023, Mar 24). Vietnam may resist diplomatic upgrade with Washington as U.S.-China tensions simmer. *Reuters*. www.msn.com/en-au/news/world/vietnam-may-resist-diplomatic-upgrade-with-washington-as-us-china-tensions-simmer/ar-AA18Zz0S?ocid=msedgntp&cvid=ff340df21e3e4cb58b8d15878dd60a96&ei=10.

Haacke, J. (2019). The concept of hedging and its application to Southeast Asia: a critique and a proposal for a modified conceptual and methodological framework. *International Relations of the Asia-Pacific*, *19*(3), 375–417.

Hai, D. T. (2017). *Vietnam and the South China Sea: Politics, Security and Legality*. London: Routledge.

Hai, D. T. (2018). Vietnam: Riding the Chinese tide. *The Pacific Review*, *31*(2), 205–220.

Hai, D. T., & Kim, H. (2017). Vietnamese perception of the power transition. In D. Walton & E. Kavalski (eds.), *Power Transition in Asia* (pp. 192–206). London: Routledge.

Haneneva, V. (2022, March 12). Zelensky obvinil NATO v otsutsutstvii smelosti [Zelensky blamed NATO for the lack of courage]. *Gazeta.ru*. www.gazeta.ru/politics/news/2022/03/12/17417077.shtml.

He, K., & Feng, H. (2023). *After Hedging: Hard Choices for the Indo-Pacific States between the US and China*. Cambridge: Cambridge University Press.

Heydarian, R. J. (2017). Tragedy of small power politics: Duterte and the shifting sands of Philippine foreign policy. *Asian Security*, *13*(3), 220–236.

Holzman, F. D. (1989). Politics and guesswork: CIA and DIA estimates of Soviet military spending. *International Security*, *14*(2), 101–131.

Huang, E., & Steger, I. (2016, October 19): 'I am Chinese': Rodrigo Duterte explained the Philippines' shift in the South China Sea to China's CCTV. *Quartz*. https://qz.com/813171/i-am-chinese-president-rodrigo-duterte-explained-the-philippines-shift-in-the-south-china-sea-to-chinas-cctv.

Hutt, D. (2024, June 21). Russia's Putin in Hanoi: What does Vietnam hope to gain? *DW News*, www.dw.com/en/russias-putin-in-hanoi-what-does-vietnam-hope-to-gain/a-69438435.

Jackson V. (2014). Power, trust, and network complexity: Three logics of hedging in Asian security. *International Relations of the Asia-Pacific*, *14* (3), 331–356.

Jervis, R. (2017). *Perception and Misperception in International Politics: New Edition*. Princeton, NJ: Princeton University Press.

Johnson, B. (2022, March 6). Boris Johnson: 6 Steps the west must take to help Ukraine right now. *The New York Times*. https://www.nytimes.com/2022/03/06/opinion/boris-johnson-russia-putin-ukraine-war.html.

Jones, D. M., & Jenne, N. (2021). Hedging and grand strategy in Southeast Asian foreign policy. *International Relations of the Asia-Pacific*. 205–235.

Jozwiak, R. (2022, October 4). Devil In The Details: Ukraine's Tricky Bid For NATO Membership. *Radio Free Europe*. www.rferl.org/a/ukraine-nato-membership-bid-analysis/32064808.html.

Kakachia, K., Nodia, G., Shelest, H. et al. (2013). *Georgian Foreign Policy: The Quest for Sustainable Security*. Tbilisi: Konrad- Adenauer-Stiftung. Retrieved 31 January 2021, from: (PDF) Georgian Foreign Policy: The Quest for Sustainable Security (researchgate.net).

Karaganov, S. (2011, June 17). Aziatskaya Strategiya [The Asian Strategy]. *Rossiiskaya Gazeta [The Russian Newspaper]*, no. 5505(129). https://rg.ru/2011/06/17/karaganov.html.

Kashin, V. (2018). Russian perspectives on the third Offset Strategy and its implications for Russian-Chinese defense technological cooperation. In T. M. Cheung & T. G. Mahnken (eds.), *The Gathering Pacific Storm: Emerging US-China Strategic Competition in Defense Technological and Industrial Development* (pp. 211–239). Amherst, New York: Cambria Press.

Klapper, B. (2012, December 6). Clinton fears efforts to 're-Sovietize' in Europe. *Associated Press*. https://apnews.com/article/06bc71ef220943978ba000620f16d022.

Klimova, A. (2022, July 16). V ofise Zelenskogo nedovol'nu novoi voennoi pomosch'yu ot NATO. 'Daleko on nashuh real'nuh nuzhd' [Zelensky's Office is unhappy with new military assistance from NATO. 'Far from our real needs']. https://ura.news/news/1052561958.

Kofman, M., & Connolly, R. (2019, 16 December). Why Russian military expenditure is much higher than commonly understood (as is China's). *War on the Rocks*. https://warontherocks.com/2019/12/why-russian-military-expenditure-is-much-higher-than-commonly-understood-as-is-chinas/.

Koga, K. (2018) The concept of 'hedging' revisited: The case of Japan's foreign policy strategy in East Asia's power shift. *International Studies Review*, *20* (4), 633–660.

Kommersant.ru (2010, April 18). Tamozhennui Souz – eto tol'ko pervui etap integratcii [The Custom Union is only the first step of integration]. www.kommersant.ru/doc/1623955.

Korolev, A. (2018). Theories of non-balancing and Russia's foreign policy. *Journal of Strategic Studies*, *41*(6), 887–912.

Korolev, A. (2019). Shrinking room for hedging: System-unit dynamics and behaviour of smaller powers. *International Relations of the Asia-Pacific*, *19*(3), 419–452.

Koshkina, S. (2015). *Maidan: Nerasskazannaya istoria [Maidan: the untold story]*. Kyiv: Bright Star.

Krasner, S. D. (1999). *Sovereignty: Organized Hypocrisy*. Princeton, NJ: Princeton University Press.

Kuik, C.C. (2008). The essence of hedging: Malaysia and Singapore's response to a rising China. *Contemporary Southeast Asia: A Journal of International and Strategic Affairs*, *30*(2), 159–185.

Kuik, C. C. (2013). Malaysia's US policy under Najib: Structural and domestic sources of a small state's strategy. *Asian Security*, *9*(3), 143–164.

Kuik, C. (2016) Malaysia between the United States and China: What do weaker states hedge against? *Asian Politics & Policy*, *8*(1), 155–177.

Kuik, C. C. (2021). Getting hedging right: A small-state perspective. *China International Strategy Review*, *3*(2), 300–315.

Kutsenko, Y. (2018). Understanding campaign 'axiotechniques': Their nature and practical usage in Ukrainian elections. *Politics in Central Europe*, *14*(1), 7–33.

Lai, Y. M., & Kuik, C. C. (2020). Structural sources of Malaysia's South China Sea policy: power uncertainties and small-state hedging. *Australian Journal of International Affairs*, *75*(3), 277–304.https://doi.org/10.1080/10357718.2020.18563291.

Lake, D. A. (1996). Anarchy, hierarchy, and the variety of international relations. *International Organization*, *50*(1), 1–33.

Lee, J. Y. (2017). Hedging strategies of the middle powers in East Asian security: The cases of South Korea and Malaysia. *East Asia*, *34*(1), 23–37.

Lijphart, A. (1971). Comparative politics and the comparative method. *American Political Science Review*, *65*, 682–693.

Lim, D. J. & Cooper, Z. (2015). Reassessing hedging: The logic of alignment in East Asia. *Security Studies*, *24*(4), 696–727.

Liu, F. 2023. Balance of power, balance of alignment, and China's role in the regional order transition. *The Pacific Review*, *36*(2), 261–283.

López i Vidal, L., & Pelegrín, A. (2018). Hedging against China: Japanese strategy towards a rising power. *Asian Security* *14*(2), 193–211.

Lowy Institute. (2021). *Asia Power Index 2021*. https://power.lowyinstitute.org/data/military-capability/defence-spending/military-expenditure-defence-sector-ppp/.

Mahbubani, K. (2017). Qatar: Big lessons from a small country [Text]. *The Straits Times*. www.straitstimes.com/opinion/qatar-big-lessons-froma-small-country.

Manila Bulletin. (2019). Lorenzana Says 67-year Old MDT Could Becme Cause, Not Deterrent, for Chaos. Manila Bulletin, 5 March, pp. 1–2.

MacFarlane, S. (2016). Georgia's security predicament. In G. Nodia (ed.), *25 Years of Independent Georgia: Achievements and Unfinished Projects* (pp. 208–236). Tbilisi: Konrad-Adenauer-Stiftung.

Marston, H. S. (2024). Navigating great power competition: A neoclassical realist view of hedging. *International Relations of the Asia-Pacific*, *24*(1), 29–63.

Mearsheimer, J. J. (2001). *The Tragedy of Great Power Politics*. New York: W. W. Norton & Company.

Medcalf, R. (2014). In defence of the Indo-Pacific: Australia's new strategic map. *Australian Journal of International Affairs*, *68*(4), 470(2018)483.

Medeiros, E. S. (2005). Strategic hedging and the future of Asia-pacific stability. *The Washington Quarterly*, *29*(1), 145–167.

Merabishvili, G. & Kiss, A. (2016). The perception of national security in Georgia. *Lithuanian Annual Strategic Review*, *14*, 159–177. De Gruyter, https://doi.org/10.1515/lasr-2016-0007.

Morgenthau, H.J. (1948). *Politics Among Nations: The Struggle for Power and Peace*. New York: Alfred A. Knopf.

Mosyakov, D. (2013). Na Grani Fola: Politika Kitaya v Yuzno-Kitaiskom More [Extremely Risk-taking: China's Behaivor in the South China Sea]. *Index Bezopasnosti [Security Index]*, *19*(4), 58–67.

Mouritzen, H., & Wivel, A. (2012). *Explaining Foreign Policy: International Diplomacy and the Russo-Georgian War*. London: Lynne Rienner.

Narizny, K. (2017). On systemic paradigms and domestic politics: A critique of the newest realism. *International Security*, *42*(2), 155–190.

National Defense Strategy Commission. 2018. *Providing for the common defense: The assessments and recommendations of the National Defense Strategy Commission*. United States Institute of Peace. www.usip.org/publications/2018/11/providing-common-defense.

NATO, (2008, April 3). Bucharest Summit Declaration, Press Release, www.nato.int/docu/pr/2008/p08-049e.html.

New Straits Times. 2021. Malaysia concerned with trilateral AUKUS security pact. www.nst.com.my/news/nation/2021/09/728403/malaysia-concerned-trilateral-aukus-security-pact. Accessed 18 September 2021.

NEWSru.com. (2012, January 2). Vmesto pozdravleniya: Rossiya pred'yavila Ukraine tamozhenno-gazovui ultimatum [Instead of a congratulation: Russia issued Ukraine a custom-gas ultimatum]. www.newsru.com/finance/02jan2013/rus_ukr.html.

Nichol, J. (2008, October 24). *Russia-Georgia Conflict in South Ossetia: Context and Implications for U.S. Interests*. Washington, DC: Congressional Research Service.

Noren, J. H. (1995). The controversy over Western measures of Soviet defense expenditures. *Post-Soviet Affairs*, *11*(3), 238–276.

Office of the President of the Philippines (2018). *National Security Strategy: Security and Development for Transformational Change and Well-being of the Filipino People*. Manila.

Ohle, M., Cook, R. J., & Han, Z. (2020). China's engagement with Kazakhstan and Russia's Zugzwang: Why is Nur-Sultan incurring regional power hedging?. *Journal of Eurasian Studies*, *11*(1), 86–103.

Osetinskii, O. (2004). Mikhail Saakashvili: Shevardnadze vsegda obmanyval Putina [Mikhail Saakashvili: Shevardnadze has always deceived Putin] *Izvestia* (12 April). http://izvestia.ru/news/289012.

Pakiam, G. K. (2019). Malaysia in 2018: The year of voting dangerously. In D. Singh & M. Cook (eds.), *Southeast Asia Affairs 2019*, (pp. 195–210). Singapore: ISEAS – Yushof Ishak Institute.

Panda, A. (2019). In Philippines, Pompeo Offers Major Alliance Assurance on South China Sea. The DIplomat, 4 March, pp. 1–2.

Perlo-freeman, S. & Solmirano, C. (2014). *Trends in World Military Expenditure, 2013*. SIPRI Factsheet. Stockholm International Peace Research Institute. www.sipri.org/sites/default/files/files/FS/SIPRIFS1404.pdf.

Peuch, J-Ch. (2004). Georgia: Saakashvili in Moscow, Looking to start ties with a clean slate. *Radio Free Europe/Radio Liberty*. Retrieved 31 January 2021, www.rferl.org/a/1051504.html.

Pop, V. (2009, March 21). EU expanding its 'sphere of influence', Russia says. *EUobserver*. https://euobserver.com/foreign/27827.

Pozner, V. (2017, November 13). Interview with Nino Burjanadze, available in Russian at www.1tv.ru/shows/pozner/vypuski/gost-nino-burdzhanadze-pozner-vypusk-ot-13-11-2017.

President of Russia. (2008, September 12). *Stenograficheskii otchet o vstreche s uchastnikami mezhdunarodnogo kluba 'Valdai' [Transcript of meeting with the participants of the Valdai discussion club]*. http://kremlin.ru/events/presi dent/transcripts/1383.

President of Russia. (2013, September 19). *Zasedanie mezhdunarodnogo dis- kussionnogo klybf 'Valdai' [The meeting of the international discussion club 'Valdai']*. http://kremlin.ru/events/president/news/19243.

President of Russia. (2014, December 26). *Voyennaya doktrina Rossiyskoy Federatsii [Military Doctrine of the Russian Federation]*. http://static.krem lin.ru/media/events/files/41d527556bec8deb3530.pdf.

President of the United States (2017, December 18). *National security strategy of the United States of America*. www.whitehouse.gov/wp-content/uploads/ 2017/12/NSS-Final-12-18-2017-0905.pdf.

Putin, V. (April, 2008). *The Russian President's Instructions to the Russian Federation Government with regard to Abkhazia and South Ossetia*. Retrieved 5 May 2021, from https://russiaun.ru/en/news/200804160419.

Radio Free Asia (2019, February 11). Malaysia's Anwar Tells Southeast Asian Nations to Defend Territory against China. www.rfa.org/english/news/china/ anwar-southeastasia-02112019174818.html.

Raik, K. (2019). The Ukraine crisis as a conflict over Europe's political, economic and security order. *Geopolitics, 24*(1), 51–70.

Ratcliffe, R (2024, June 20). Russia and Vietnam agree to strengthen ties during Putin state visit. *The Guardian*, www.theguardian.com/world/article/2024/ jun/20/vladimir-putin-vietnam-state-visit.

Regnum (2008, August 14). Tragediya Saakashvili: Reputaciya SSHA padaet [The tragedy of Saakashvili: USA's reputation is declining], https://regnum .ru/news/polit/1041323.html.

Ripsman, N. M. (2009). Neoclassical realism and domestic interest groups. In S. E. Lobell, N. M. Ripsman, & J. W. Taliaferro (eds.), *Neoclassical Realism, the State, and Foreign Policy* (pp. 170–193). Cambridge: Cambridge University Press.

Ripsman, N. M., Taliaferro, J. W., & Lobell, S. E. (2016). *Neoclassical Realist Theory of International Politics*. Oxford University Press.

Romero, A. (2019). Palace: Arbitral Ruling 'Never Shelved'. The Philippine Star, 14 April. www.philstar.com/headlines/2019/04/14/1909998/palace-arbi tral-ruling-never-shelved.

RT. (2008, July 9). Condoleezza Rice: U.S. backs Georgia. www.rt.com/news/ condoleezza-rice-us-backs-georgia/.

RT. (2013, August 19). Trade 'suicide': Russia prepares to tighten borders if Ukraine signs on with EU. www.rt.com/business/trade-war-ukraine-russia-656/.

Saakashvili, M. (January 24, 2004). Inauguration Speech. Retrieved 1 May 2021, from https://old.civil.ge/eng/article.php?id=26694.

Sidorenko, S., & Kolesnikov, A. (2013, May 30). Mezhdu soyuzom i sovetom [Between the union and the Council], *Kommersant*. www.kommersant.ru/doc/2200231.

Sizov, V. (2009). Piatidnevka Protivostoyaniya [Five days of confrontation]. *International Trends*, 6(2), 116–122.

Smith, D. (2009, June 2). Georgia the key to US-Russia 'Reset'. *Atlantic Council*. www.atlanticcouncil.org/blogs/new-atlanticist/georgia-the-key-to-usrussia-reset/.

Smith, N. R. (2018). Strategic Hedging by Smaller Powers: What can Neoclassical Realism Add? Paper prepared for the Workshop: Re-Appraising Neoclassical Realism, London School of Economics, 29 November 2018.

Smith, N. R. (2020). When hedging goes wrong: Lessons from Ukraine's failed hedge of the EU and Russia. *Global Policy*, 11(5), 588–597.

Snyder, G. H. (1984). The security dilemma in alliance politics. *World Politics*, 36(4), 461–495.

Sokirko, V. (2022, March 5). Prezident Zelenskii absolutno prav. NATO ispugalos' [President Zelensky is absolutely right. NATO got scared. *TASS News Agency*. www.gazeta.ru/army/2022/03/05/14603557.shtml?updated.

Sokov, N. (2005). *The Withdrawal of Russian Military Bases from Georgia: Not Solving Anything*. PONARS Policy Memo 363, Monterey Institute of International Studies. Retrieved 15 May 2021, from www.ponarseurasia.org/wpcontent/uploads/attachments/pm_0363.pdf.

Stein, J. G. (2013). Threat perception in international relations. In L. Huddy, D. O. Sears, and J. S. Levy (eds.), *The Oxford Handbook of Political Psychology*, 2nd ed. (online ed., Oxford Academic, 16 December 2013), https://doi.org/10.1093/oxfordhb/9780199760107.013.0012, accessed 28 January 2025.

Stelzenmüller, C. (2010, September 27). Walk – But Learn to Chew the Gum Too. *The Green Political Foundation*. www.boell.de/en/navigation/europe-transatlantic-transatlantic-approaches-new-eastern-policy-10236.html.

Strangio, S. (2024, June 21). Following Putin Visit, Senior US Official Touches Down in Vietnam. *The Diplomat*, https://thediplomat.com/2024/06/following-putin-visit-senior-us-official-touches-down-in-vietnam/.

Strating, R. (2022). Norm contestation, statecraft and the South China Sea: Defending maritime order. *The Pacific Review*, 35(1), 1–31.

Sumsky, V. (2012). Rossiya i Problemu Yuzhno-Kitaiskogo Moria [Russia and the Problems of the South China Sea]. Govoriat Expertu MGIMO [MGIMO Experts are Speaking], 3 May. https://mgimo.ru/about/news/experts/223482/.

Suzuki A., & Lee P. P. (2017). Malaysia's hedging strategy, a rising China, and the changing strategic situation in East Asia. In L. Dittmer & C. B. Ngeow (eds.), *Southeast Asia and China: A Contest in Mutual Socialization*, (pp. 113–129). Singapore: World Scientific.

TASS. (2021, September 2). Russia, Vietnam Aim for Further Promotion of Partnership — Statement. https://tass.com/politics/1368907.

TASS. (2022a, March 5). Zelenskii nazval vstrechy glav MID stran NATO v Brussele slaboi [Zelensky calls the meeting of NATO foreign affairs ministers in Brussels weak]. https://tass.ru/mezhdunarodnaya-panorama/13971851?utm_source=google.com&utm_medium=organic&utm_campaign=google.com&utm_referrer=google.com.

TASS. (2022b, March 15). Zelenskii zayavil o neobhodimosti priznat, chto Ukraine ne voiti v NATO [Zelensky stated a necessity to admit that Ukraine will not join NATO]. https://tass.ru/mezhdunarodnaya-panorama/14076053.

Tessman, B. F. (2012). System structure and state strategy: Adding hedging to the menu. *Security Studies, 21*(2), 192–231.

Tessman, B., & Wolfe, W. (2011). Great powers and strategic hedging: The case of Chinese energy security strategy. *International Studies Review, 13*(2), 214–240.

The White House (2009, February 7). *Remarks by Vice President Biden at 45th Munich Conference on Security Policy*. https://obamawhitehouse.archives.gov/the-press-office/remarks-vice-president-biden-45th-munich-conference-security-policy.

Thayer, C. A. (2002). Vietnamese perspectives of the 'China threat'. In I. Storey & H. Yee (eds.), *The China Threat: Perceptions, Myths and Reality*, (pp. 270–292). London: Routledge.

Thayer, C. A. (2017). Vietnam's foreign policy in an era of rising Sino-US competition and increasing domestic political influence. *Asian Security, 13*(3), 183–199.

Tolstrup, J. (2014). *Russia vs. the EU: The Competition for Influence in Post-Soviet States*. Boulder, CO: First Forum Press. Boulder (Colo.).

Torode, G. (2011). Beijing Pressure Intense in South China Sea Row. South China Morning Post, 23 September. www.scmp.com/article/979876/beijing-pressure-intense-south-china-sea-row.

Tu, C. C., Tien, H. P., & Hwang, J. J. (2024). Untangling threat perception in international relations: An empirical analysis of threats posed by China and their implications for security discourse. *Cogent Arts & Humanities, 11*(1), 1–31. https://doi.org/10.1080/23311983.2024.2335766.

Tunsjø, Ø. (2013). *Security and profit in China's energy policy: Hedging against risk*. Columbia University Press.

UKRINFORM. (2013, February 25). Barroso reminds Ukraine that Customs Union and free trade with EU are incompatible. www.ukrinform.net/rubric-economy/1461921-barroso_reminds_ukraine_that_customs_union_and_free_trade_with_eu_are_incompatible_299321.html.

USINDOPACOM. (2019, October 1). China's Challenge to a Free and Open Indo-Pacific. *US Indo-Pacific Command*. https://www.pacom.mil/Media/Speeches-Testimony/Article/1976518/chinas-challenge-to-a-free-and-open-indo-pacific/.

US Department of Defence (2021, October 17). *Secretary of Defense Travels to Europe to Reassure Front Line States*. www.defense.gov/News/News-Stories/Article/Article/2812786/secretary-of-defense-travels-to-europe-to-reassure-front-line-states/.

U.S. Senate Armed Services Committee. (2018). *Department of Defense Authorization for Appropriations for Fiscal Year 2019 and the Future Years Defense Program. U.S. Government Publishing Office*. https://www.govinfo.gov/content/pkg/CHRG-115shrg42143/html/CHRG-115shrg42143.htm.

VietnamNet. (2016, Octobre 26). Relations with CPV Critical to Boosting US–Vietnam Ties: John Kerry.

Viray, P. L. (2018) Singaporean envoy: ASEAN unable to resolve South China Sea row. Philstar.Com. www.philstar.com/news-commentary/2018/04/03/1802429/opinion.

Waltz, K. (1979). *Theory of International Politics*. Boston, Mass: McGraw-Hill.

Wezeman, S. T. (2020, April 27). Russia's military spending: Frequently asked questions. SIPRI Factsheet. Stockholm International Peace Research Institute. https://www.sipri.org/commentary/topical-backgrounder/2020/russias-military-spending-frequently-asked-questions#:~:text=Converting%20Russian%20military%20expenditure%20using,billion%20using%20market%20exchange%20rates.

White House. (2022). *The Indo Pacific strategy of the United States*. February 2022. www.whitehouse.gov/wp-content/uploads/2022/02/U.S.-Indo-Pacific-Strategy.pdf.

Wilkins, T. (2021). Middle power hedging in the era of security/economic disconnect: Australia, Japan, and the 'Special Strategic Partnership'. *International Relations of the Asia-Pacific. 23*(1), 93–127.

Wolfers, A. (1952). "National security" as an ambiguous symbol. *Political Science Quarterly, 67*(4), 481–502.

World Bank. (2019). [World Bank national accounts data, and OECD National Accounts data files]. Retrieved 10 November 2020, from https://data.worldbank.org/indicator/NY.GDP.MKTP.CD?locations=CN-RU-US-IN&most_recent_year_desc=false.

Zerkalo nedeli. (2012, November 13). Posol Ukrainy v RF nazval usloviya vstupleniya v Tamozhennyi soyuz [Ukraine's ambassador in Russia named conditions of joining the Customs Union]. https://zn.ua/ECONOMICS/posol_ukrainy_v_rf_nazval_usloviya_vstupleniya_v_tamozhennyy_soyuz.html.

Zhang, F. (2020). China's long march at sea: Explaining Beijing's South China Sea strategy, 2009–2016. *The Pacific Review, 33*(5), 757–787.

Cambridge Elements

International Relations

Series Editors

Jon C. W. Pevehouse
University of Wisconsin–Madison

Jon C. W. Pevehouse is the Mary Herman Rubinstein Professor of Political Science and Public Policy at the University of Wisconsin–Madison. He has published numerous books and articles in IR in the fields of international political economy, international organizations, foreign policy analysis, and political methodology. He is a former editor of the leading IR field journal, International Organization.

Tanja A. Börzel
Freie Universität Berlin

Tanja A. Börzel is the Professor of political science and holds the Chair for European Integration at the Otto-Suhr-Institute for Political Science, Freie Universität Berlin. She holds a PhD from the European University Institute, Florence, Italy. She is coordinator of the Research College "The Transformative Power of Europe," as well as the FP7-Collaborative Project "Maximizing the Enlargement Capacity of the European Union" and the H2020 Collaborative Project "The EU and Eastern Partnership Countries: An Inside-Out Analysis and Strategic Assessment." She directs the Jean Monnet Center of Excellence "Europe and its Citizens."

Edward D. Mansfield
University of Pennsylvania

Edward D. Mansfield is the Hum Rosen Professor of Political Science, University of Pennsylvania. He has published well over 100 books and articles in the area of international political economy, international security, and international organizations. He is Director of the Christopher H. Browne Center for International Politics at the University of Pennsylvania and former program co-chair of the American Political Science Association.

Editorial Team

International Relations Theory
Jeffrey T. Checkel, European University Institute, Florence

International Political Economy
Edward D. Mansfield, University of Pennsylvania
Stefanie Walter, University of Zurich

International Security
Jon C. W. Pevehouse, University of Wisconsin–Madison

International Organisations
Tanja A. Börzel, Freie Universität Berlin

About the Series

The Cambridge Elements Series in International Relations publishes original research on key topics in the field. The series includes manuscripts addressing international security, international political economy, international organizations, and international relations.

Cambridge Elements

International Relations

Elements in the Series

Digital Globalization: Politics, Policy, and a Governance Paradox
Stephen Weymouth

After Hedging: Hard Choices for the Indo-Pacific States between the US and China
Kai He and Huiyun Feng

IMF Lending: Partisanship, Punishment, and Protest
M. Rodwan Abouharb and Bernhard Reinsberg

Building Pathways to Peace: State–Society Relations and Security Sector Reform
Nadine Ansorg and Sabine Kurtenbach

Drones, Force and Law: European Perspectives
David Hastings Dunn and Nicholas J. Wheeler

The Selection and Tenure of Foreign Ministers Around the World
Hanna Bäck, Alejandro Quiroz Flores and Jan Teorell

Lockean Liberalism in International Relations
Alexandru V. Grigorescu and Claudio J. Katz

Tip-toeing through the Tulips with Congress: How Congressional Attention Constrains Covert Action
Dani Kaufmann Nedal and Madison V. Schramm

Social Cues: How the Liberal Community Legitimizes Humanitarian War
Jonathan A. Chu

Environmental Ethics of War
Tamar Meisels

Norms, Practices, and Social Change in Global Politics
Steven Bernstein, Aarie Glas and Marion Laurence

When Hedging Fails: Structural Uncertainty, Protective Options, and Geopolitical (Im)Prudence in Smaller Powers' Behaviour
Alexander Korolev

A full series listing is available at: www.cambridge.org/EIR

For EU product safety concerns, contact us at Calle de José Abascal, 56–1°, 28003 Madrid, Spain or eugpsr@cambridge.org.

www.ingramcontent.com/pod-product-compliance
Lightning Source LLC
LaVergne TN
LVHW011857060526
838200LV00054B/4388